Parenting
Gifted
Children.
101

An Introduction to Gifted Kids
and Their Needs

Parenting
Gifted
Children
101

Tracy Ford Inman, Ed.D.,
& Jana Kirchner, Ph.D.

Routledge
Taylor & Francis Group

NEW YORK AND LONDON

First published in 2016 by Prufrock Press Inc.

Published in 2021 by Routledge
605 Third Avenue, New York, NY 10017
4 Park Square, Milton Park, Abingdon, Oxon OX14 4RN

Routledge is an imprint of the Taylor & Francis Group, an informa business

Copyright © 2016 by Taylor & Francis Group

Cover design by Raquel Trevino and layout design by Allegra Denbo

ISBN 13: 978-1-61821-518-5 (pbk)

DOI: 10.4324/9781003237013

Library of Congress Cataloging-in-Publication Data

Names: Inman, Tracy F. (Tracy Ford), 1963- author. | Kirchner, Jana, author.
Title: Parenting gifted children 101 : an introduction to gifted kids and
  their needs / by Tracy Ford Inman, Ed.D, and Jana Kirchner, Ph.D.
Description: Waco, Texas : Prufrock Press Inc., 2016.
Identifiers: LCCN 2016007464| ISBN 9781618215185 (pbk.)
Subjects: LCSH: Gifted children. | Parents of gifted children. | Parenting. |
  Gifted children--Education. | Education--Parent participation.
Classification: LCC HQ773.5 .I66 2016 | DDC 305.9/089083--dc23
LC record available at https://lccn.loc.gov/2016007464

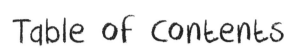

Table of Contents

Acknowledgements

We would like to extend our deepest gratitude to all the administrators, teachers, and parents who took the time to respond to our survey questions and share their insights about gifted children. We feel their stories and experiences are a major strength of our book! Special thanks to Toddie Adams, Angie Barrandeguy, David Baxter, Constance Baynum, Amy Berry, Karen Bickett, Cecelia Boswell, Lynette Breedlove, Jane Bush, Dina Chaffin, Jennifer Chaplin, Debbie Dailey, Anita Davis, Keith Davis, Mary Evans, LaTonya Frazier, Gregory Grey, Tracy Harkins, Claire Hughes, Leslie Hutchinson, Ruth Kertis, Laureen Laumeyer, Andrew McMichael, Jane Paulin, Pam Petty, Mary Cay Ricci, Jennifer Sheffield, Cathleen Skidmore, Kandy Smith, Deborah Strubler, Penny Teague, Kelli Thompson, Melissa Wassom, and Tim Wilson. We are also grateful to Lynette Breedlove, Mary Evans, Leslie Hutchinson, Jenny Robins, and Mary Young for reading the manuscript in progress and providing feedback.

A heartfelt thank you goes to the amazing students that both of us have taught over the last 20-plus years. You challenged us, made us laugh, helped us develop as teachers (and human beings), and learned with us. Many of your stories are examples in this book.

Most importantly, we thank our families who supported and encouraged us during this project. A special thank you goes to our children (Jake and Zach Inman, Caleb and Caitlyn Kirchner) who inspired many of the stories in this book as we figured out how to answer your many questions as preschoolers, to support and encourage your gifts and talents through elementary school, and to nurture and challenge you through your teen and young adult years. We are honored to be your moms and are in awe of the people you have become.

Introduction: Tips for Reading This Book

> Failure to help the gifted child reach his potential is a societal tragedy, the extent of which is difficult to measure but what is surely great. How can we measure the sonata unwritten, the curative drug undiscovered, the absence of political insight? They are the difference between what we are and what we could be as a society. (Gallagher, 1975, p. 9)

We couldn't agree more with Jim Gallagher, one of gifted education's patriarchs, so our goal for this book is to help you as parents help your gifted child reach her potential. With that as our focus, we have created a practical, user-friendly book designed to provide information and to empower you to be an effective advocate for your child. Each chapter targets an essential question and answers it with background information, current research, useful tips, connections to home and school, and additional resources. Most importantly, we include insights, stories, and advice from dozens of parents, teachers, and administrators who have experience with gifted children. Unless otherwise noted, these quotes come from parents of gifted children, teachers working directly with gifted children, and district gifted coordinators. Some have dual roles, such as a parent and a teacher. We hope that these authentic voices not only connect on a personal level with you but also teach you important lessons about parenting your gifted child.

You can read this book in a couple of ways—from beginning to end or by picking and choosing chapters that address your most pressing questions. Chapters 1–6 contain implications for home and school, prac-

DOI: 10.4324/9781003237013-1

tical applications of the concepts discussed, at the end of the chapters. The entire focus of Chapters 7 and 8, entitled *How Can I Communicate and Partner With My Child's Educators?* and *What Can I Do at Home to Help My Child?*, however, is an in-depth discussion of implications for school and home. Each chapter also includes a section called *For More Information*, describing additional print and online resources related to that topic. Full web addresses for any websites mentioned in the chapter are provided. We have also included a glossary so that you have a quick way to define terms when needed.

Our hope is that you will use this book and the additional resources we mention to guide you as you parent your gifted and talented child. Yes, you will face challenges along the way, but you will also experience laughter, joy, and awe as your child develops into the person he could be—whether that is (as in Jim Gallagher's vision) a composer, medical researcher, political leader, or something altogether different.

chapter 1

What Does Gifted Mean?

Parents of gifted children should learn all they can about giftedness, be engaged in their students' lives, be advocates for their
children in schools, be intentional about finding appropriate
services outside of the school, and above all, be cautious about
their social and emotional needs. That's a tall order, huh?
—Jennifer Chaplin, district coordinator

Either your child (or a young person significant in your life) has
been identified as gifted or you suspect that he is—otherwise you
wouldn't be reading this. In order to understand and appreciate the
specifics of social-emotional needs, appropriate learning experiences,
effective communication with educators, and all of the other critical
topics explored in this book, you need to understand some basics first:
what *gifted* means, the areas of giftedness and identification for each,
legislation and policies that affect gifted children, and the rights of
gifted children.

Definition

Depending on whom you ask, the phrase *gifted and talented* can
take on a plethora of meanings. The phrase is always evolving, but,
ultimately, the most important definitions to know are your state's and
district's interpretations of *gifted and talented* because those interpretations directly affect your child's education. In order to have a deeper

DOI: 10.4324/9781003237013-2

understanding, however, a brief look at well-known definitions proves helpful.

Founding leader in gifted education Joe Renzulli (1978), for example, argued that ability is only one part of gifted behavior—one also needs motivation and creativity. Francoys Gagné (1985), another early scholar, differentiated between gifts, which are natural abilities, and talents, which are intentionally developed from gifts. Three contemporary thinkers in the field, Rena Subotnik, Paula Olszewski-Kubilius, and Frank Worrell (2011), examined a century of research in order to redefine *giftedness* as:

> the manifestation of performance or production that is clearly at the upper end of the distribution in a talent domain even relative to that of other high-functioning individuals in that domain. Further, giftedness can be viewed as developmental, in that in the beginning stages, potential is the key variable; in later stages, achievement is the measure of giftedness; and in fully developed talents, eminence is the basis on which this label is granted. Psychosocial variables play an essential role in the manifestation of giftedness at every developmental stage. Both cognitive and psychosocial variables are malleable and need to be deliberately cultivated. (p. 7)

Potential and ability alone, according to this approach, do not designate giftedness. One must produce or perform at exceptionally high levels compared to others talented in the area.

Although leaders in the field of gifted education hold differing views of giftedness, the federal definition is very clear. The definition in the Marland Report (1972), the first national report on giftedness, which was developed to increase America's global competitiveness, defined gifted and talented children as those with "outstanding abilities, (who) are capable of high performance" (p. ix). It argued these children needed differentiated learning experiences in order to thrive. That federal definition has been honed over the years to read this way:

The term "gifted and talented" . . . means students, children, or youth who give evidence of high achievement capability in such areas as intellectual, creative, artistic, or leadership capacity, or in specific academic fields, and who need services or activities not ordinarily provided by the school in order to fully develop those capabilities. (Every Student Succeeds Act, 2015, Title IX, Part A, Definition 22)

The most important definition for your child, however, is your state's definition of *giftedness*. The National Association for Gifted Children (NAGC) posts individual state information on its website (see For More Information). Regardless of the definition used, children and youth with gifts and talents are exceptional students who learn differently from the norm. They require services and accommodations in traditional school settings in order to thrive and have continuous progress in their learning and growth.

Areas of Giftedness

Although most people envision a young person with a high Intelligence Quotient (IQ) when they think of a gifted child, intellectual ability is only one area of giftedness. (IQ numerically represents the general intelligence of a person; it stems from standardized tests.) The Marland Report (1972) listed six areas of giftedness: "1. general intellectual ability, 2. specific academic aptitude, 3. creative or productive thinking, 4. leadership ability, 5. visual and performing arts, 6. psychomotor ability" (p. ix). Contemporary classifications typically exclude the psychomotor area because so many schools do a beautiful job developing talent in their athletes. Your child can be identified in any one of these areas, but she may also be identified in any combination. Realize, too, that although traditional measures are mentioned for identification in the descriptions below, no one measure should be used for identification, and the measure should be appropriate. Imagine the English language learner (ELL) who doesn't speak English well taking a verbal or written test in English to determine his giftedness or the talented musician taking a pen-and-paper test to see if she qualifies as gifted in music.

General Intellectual Ability

These children have the ability to do well in all areas (note that having the ability does not necessarily mean they are performing well in all areas). Typically their IQ is at least 130 (with 100 being norm). Figure 1.1 shows a normal curve for IQ. The vertical lines on the figure represent standard deviation, which is a number indicating how widely individuals in a group vary; in this figure, the standard deviation is 15 IQ points. Taking 100 as the normal or average, if you look at one standard deviation each way, people with 85 to 115 IQ have average IQs—roughly 68% of the population. Moving left, two standard deviations take us to 70; approximately 13.6% of the population has IQs that fall between 70 and 85. Only a little more than 2% score between 70 and 55. Students who have IQs below 70 qualify for special education with substantial federal funds. People with IQs of three standard deviations (i.e., 55) and below (.1% of the population) are rarely in a regular classroom and have significant assistance, sometimes a one-on-one aide. Now move to the right side of the 100. The numbers parallel: 13.6% score between 115 and 130 while 2% score between 130 and 145, which is two standard deviations from the norm; 130 IQ is typically considered the cut-off point for giftedness. Note that less than .1% scores above 145. In total, less than 3% of the population falls into this category, which, on the graph, is two or more standard deviations. However, unlike the mirrored-image counterparts (the 2-plus% scoring 70 or below), there is no federal funding for direct services to these children. (Services are educational options designed to address the needs, interests, and abilities of the student; these include everything from differentiation in the regular classroom, acceleration, dual credit, independent study, and more. Chapter 5 provides detailed information.) The vast majority of gifted children are sitting in a regular classroom without significant modifications and services. Figure 1.2 may simplify the concept of IQ range for you; it includes descriptors that interpret what that range means for each population. Please don't think of the

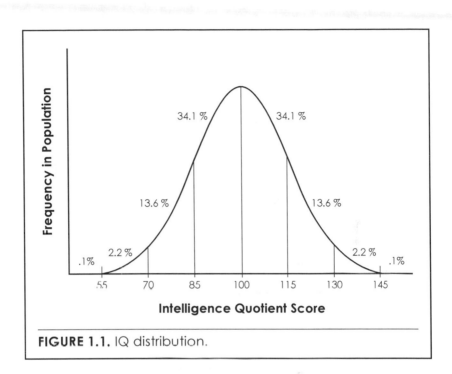

FIGURE 1.1. IQ distribution.

IQ	Approximate percentage of the population with this IQ	Interpretation
> 145	0.1	Highly gifted
130–145	2.2	Gifted
115–130	13.6	Above average intelligence
85–115	68.2	Average intelligence
70–85	13.6	Below average intelligence
55–70	2.2	Cognitively impaired
< 55	0.1	Severely impaired

FIGURE 1.2. IQ range interpretation.

descriptors as categorizing children; rather, think of them as starting points to help address the needs of your child.

Specific Academic Aptitude

Children can be identified in one or more specific academic areas: math, language arts, science, and social studies. Specific academic aptitude describes, for example, the fourth grader working at the seventh-grade level in math but still at the fourth-grade level in reading. Of course, identification stipulations differ by state, but traditionally a score in the 9th stanine on an achievement test will identify a student as gifted. (Standardized tests can be measured in stanines, a 9-point scale with 5 being average, so a 9th stanine score means it falls roughly into the top 4–5% of those taking an achievement test at the same time nationally.) Students may be gifted in one area but at grade level—or even below grade level—in another area.

Leadership or Psychosocial Ability

Students identified in leadership have the ability and capacity to lead others. Leadership potential can be seen during recess in the kindergartner who quickly organizes a game, appointing roles to others and ensuring that the game runs smoothly. Or it could be the middle schooler who runs a lucrative drug operation with others working for him. Leaders can be positive or negative change agents. No one test identifies a leader although there are checklists and surveys. Many schools use portfolios as part of the identification process.

Creativity

These students are creative thinkers but not necessarily creative producers such as artists (that's the next category). Children gifted in creativity look at the world differently from most; they are innovative and inventive. For example, a creative student's answer to a question may initially baffle a teacher because the child has deviated from linear thinking, coming up with a response that the teacher never even considered. Likewise, this student may suggest alternate ways of learning or of showing the teacher how she learned. Consider the sophomore in high school who marked out the teacher's essay prompt and wrote her own in order to show her thinking about the topic! Tests do exist for creativity (sounds ironic, doesn't it?), but often schools couple portfolios with the tests in order to identify students gifted in creativity.

Visual and Performing Arts

These children are the dancers, musicians, actors, singers, composers, painters, sculptors, and artists. Consider the 9-year-old singing "The Star-Spangled Banner" at a Saint Louis Cardinals game, the Broadway cast of *Matilda*, or Clara in *The Nutcracker*. Often portfolios and auditions are the main parts of the identification process.

Remember that each of these areas requires different services. Acceleration in math may be a wonderful strategy for someone identified as gifted in math, for example, but have devastating results for someone gifted in creativity. The key is matching the service to the area of giftedness and child. Resource teacher Jane Paulin commented, "Some students are gifted in nonacademic areas. If they are gifted in leadership or arts, even creativity, you may not see their reading or math scores go up even if I work with them every week." That may seem obvious, but many people mistakenly believe that if a person is gifted in one area, he is gifted in all.

> "Teachers need to understand that gifted students truly are unique and need individualized instruction just as much as other exceptional students."
> —Gregory Grey, middle school teacher and parent

Legislation, Regulations, and Policies

A crucial part of understanding what *gifted* means is knowing the legislation, regulations, and policies that affect gifted children nationally, as well as in your state and district.

National Policies

Children with exceptionalities other than giftedness (such as learning disabilities, dyslexia, or blindness) have more than $12 billion in federal funding allocated toward appropriate educational opportunities for them. Additionally, the Individuals with Disabilities Education Act (IDEA; 2004) defines who those students are, what appropriate education means, and the services to ensure their education. There is no federal legislation like IDEA for gifted children. The only federal monies slated specifically for the gifted are through the Jacob K. Javits Gifted and Talented Education Act and have ranged from $11.2 million to $0 since its original passage in 1988 (*Javits Act*, 2014). This act does not address rights for the gifted. Its focus is on research and best practice, allocating funds to National Research and Development Center for the Education of Gifted and Talented Children and Youth and competitive research grants.

Just as the Elementary and Secondary Education Act of 1965 was reauthorized and transformed into the No Child Left Behind Act (NCLB), NCLB was reauthorized and revised as the Every Student Succeeds Act (ESSA) in 2015. Thanks to great advocacy efforts, ESSA has important provisions that support learners who are gifted and talented. Not only does the act include the Javits Gifted and Talented Students Education Program, but it also adds stipulations that districts and states record the achievement data of high-achieving students on their state and district report cards. Previously, the reporting only consisted of students reaching proficiency and below, plus students from subgroups, such as ELLs. Being held accountable in such a public way brings attention and importance to gifted children and their achievement—or lack of achievement. Another huge step for gifted education is the expanded use of professional development funds that come from Title II, which dedicates monies to teacher quality:

> In applying for Title II professional development funds, states must include information about how they plan to improve the skills of teachers and other school leaders that will enable them to identify gifted and talented students and provide instruction based on the students' needs. (NAGC, 2015b, p. 1)

As well as states, districts that use this federal money for teacher professional development must apply it to meeting the needs of all learners, specifically listing gifted and talented learners as part of the all. Another provision addresses Title I funds, which are designated to schools that have high percentages of students from low socioeconomic backgrounds in order to increase achievement. Now these monies can be used to identify and serve gifted and talented students from those backgrounds. Title I and Title II funds are billions of dollars. No additional funding was granted to gifted and talented learners through ESSA; legislators simply made existing funds available to gifted students—which can have an incredible impact. This legislation is powerful. Be sure that your district understands ESSA's ramifications for gifted students.

State Policies

Legislation as to identification and services, however, falls to the states themselves. States' requirements for gifted and talented education range from identification and services in five areas to identification and service in one area only (such as general intellectual ability) to absolutely nothing. And the funding amounts differ as well—from $0 (which may include states that mandate identification and services) to more than $100 million. Only four states fully fund their gifted mandates—and 12 provide no funding at all (NAGC, 2015a). Check the NAGC website for information on your state. It's also important that you understand the components of your state's laws and regulations. For example, is there an individual education plan mandated for gifted students (i.e., a plan that matches the learning opportunities to the child's needs, interests, and abilities)? Do teachers in your state require certification in order to work with gifted students? What are the laws concerning early entrance to kindergarten? (This question becomes very important for a 4-year-old who is reading fluently and ready for formalized learning.) When does identification occur? Is there a policy for appeals or grievances?

District Policies

District policies, whether they are targeted for gifted and talented learners or not, may greatly impact them. At times, this is positive for gifted students—such as an early graduation policy intended to lower the number of dropouts that actually encourages some able students to start college at an earlier age. Some, however, unintentionally harm gifted students, such as restricting students to two online classes throughout their time in a district or requiring a certain amount of hours of seat time to earn credit for a class. Most districts have their policies on their web pages. If not, ask for a copy of the policies—it's your right as a citizen. Also ask the district's gifted coordinator about funding: Does this district add additional monies? If so, how is the funding allocated? Equally important are the procedures the school has in place to follow the district policies:

+ Does the school cluster group students? (Hopefully yes.)
+ Are there enrichment classes offered? (Hopefully yes.)
+ Are students required to do the work missed during a pull-out class? (Hopefully no.)

Chapter 5 addresses all of these services.

"I wish administrators recognized that gifted kids are many of the doctors, lawyers, scientists, teachers, and politicians of the future. They need to be challenged so that as future leaders they will be up to the task of competing internationally."

—Kandy Smith, former principal and parent

Rights

Regardless of the laws in your state or the policies and procedures in your school district, understand that your child has certain fundamental rights as a gifted child, as argued by former NAGC president

Del Siegle. During his tenure as president (2007–2009), he created the Gifted Children's Bill of Rights. As a gifted child, you have a right to:

+ know about your giftedness.
+ learn something new every day.
+ be passionate about your talent area without apologies.
+ have an identity beyond your talent area.
+ feel good about your accomplishments.
+ make mistakes.
+ seek guidance in the development of your talent.
+ have multiple peer groups and a variety of friends.
+ choose which of your talent areas you wish to pursue.
+ not be gifted at everything. (2007)

As you read each of these, consider the social, emotional, and cognitive impact of their message. This Bill of Rights should make for interesting discussion around the dinner table as well as around a school conference table.

Final Thoughts

You're reading this book in order to better understand your child and better help him in life's journey. The most powerful tool you can have in your advocacy toolkit is knowledge. Once you understand the regulations, policies, and procedures of your state, district, and school, you can be a stronger advocate for your child.

Implications for Home

+ Consider your own definition of giftedness versus the ones mentioned in this chapter. Most importantly, think about how your definition compares to your state or district's definition.
+ Join your local, state, and national gifted advocacy organizations. Find out as much information as possible. Be an advocate for all children. (See Chapter 7 for more information.)

+ Discuss the Gifted Children's Bill of Rights with your child. Talk each point through carefully. This is a wonderful foundation for teaching your child self-advocacy.

The question isn't whether to tell your child he is gifted or not; rather, it is how to tell your child. Barbara Kerr (2015), a psychologist specializing in gifted education, suggested that you follow these five steps:

1. Be specific. For example, you scored 95% in math on an achievement test. That means if 100 people of your age were in a room and took the test, then you would have scored higher than 95 of them.
2. Emphasize that the score is simply a snapshot of where your child is now. Explain that your child has been successful in the past and probably will be in the future as long as she works hard.
3. Make sure your child understands she has a responsibility to develop that talent to do good to help others.
4. It's not enough to be bright, but it's important for him to be compassionate with others, especially those who may not act in a way he thinks is right.
5. Encourage your child to make plans. Ask what he wants to do and what he thinks he needs to develop that talent.

Implications for School

+ Many state gifted advocacy organizations have institutional memberships. Consider gifting one to your child's school. It lasts a lot longer than a mug of candies or a Starbucks gift card for the holidays—and can potentially empower your child's educators. Benefits differ according to the state, but typically your child's educator would get the latest information about best practices in gifted education as well as reduced registration for conferences.

+ Find out all you can about the policies and procedures for your child's school district and school. Be aware of the district and school's responsibilities so that you can better partner with them. Many districts post their gifted policy handbooks online. If not, call or e-mail. You may want to compare these policies and procedures to your state's mandates. Find out what you can about identification and services. The more you know, the more you can advocate for your child, and the better you can partner with the school.

+ Share the Gifted Children's Bill of Rights with your child's school.

For More Information

+ Research your state's legislation and regulations regarding gifted students. Visit NAGC's "Gifted By State" (http://www. nagc.org/resources-publications/gifted-state) for detailed information.

+ Another wonderful resource is your state's gifted advocacy organization. The above NAGC web page also lists those organizations along with contact information and websites. Many state association websites list the regulations and other important information.

+ Also go to the website for your state's department of education and search for *gifted*. If you don't have luck, e-mail or call. You must know your rights and your child's rights in order to be an effective advocate.

chapter 2

What Are the Myths About Gifted Children?

There are a lot of teachers that still believe smart students are the ones that are obedient and complete all their assignments. It is difficult to get them to understand that the biggest troublemaker in their classroom might be the most gifted. It is also difficult to get them to understand how much gifted students can struggle with executive functioning such as self-regulation and flexibility.

—Tracy Harkins, parent

One of the greatest issues facing gifted education is its thriving mythology. From grade acceleration being emotionally and socially scarring (it's not) to using the gifted child as a tutor (a poor educational choice), misunderstandings run rampant. This chapter explores some of the most damaging ones.

The Myths

All children are gifted.

This is a tough one because those who refute it sound elitist. The simple truth is that all children are not gifted (see Chapter 1). All children are indeed special. All children possess strengths and weaknesses. All children have potential. All children are certainly worthy—worthy of love and worthy of learning. All children deserve to be appropriately challenged in school, to learn something new every day. However, chil-

DOI: 10.4324/9781003237013-3

dren with gifts and talents learn very differently from the norm; they "need services or activities not ordinarily provided by the school in order to fully develop those capabilities" as stipulated in Every Student Succeeds Act (2015; Title IX, Part A, Definition 22).

Gifted kids can get by on their own (and its counterpart: It's more important for educators to support struggling learners than advanced learners).

As the United States devoted decades to getting children to proficiency under NCLB, so many high-ability and gifted children languished. The Fordham Institute's study *High-Achieving Students in the Era of NCLB* (Loveless, Farkas, & Duffett, 2008) found the achievement gap was indeed lessening in the almost 10 years of the law—by the low achievers moving up to meet the almost stagnant top achievers. This same report indicated that teachers spend the majority of their time with the lowest achieving students, in spite of the fact that they believe all children deserve attention. It also stated that teachers "believe that academically advanced students are not a high priority in their schools" (p. 51).

At the root of this is the myth that gifted students can get by on their own. Regional coordinator Kelli Thompson wished administrators realized that these students "do need adult guidance to learn. They will not just get it on their own. If so, they could just stay home." Intellectually gifted students learn at a faster pace than their classmates, for example, sometimes needing two repetitions of a math concept instead of 30. Not only do they process concepts more quickly, but they also make complex connections. In fact, their brains physiologically differ from others—from the speed of internal connectivity in the brain to what parts of the brain are used (Jensen, 2006).

"Gifted children will not 'just get it' if they are left alone. Many times gifted children are left to fend for themselves while teachers and resources are focused on struggling learners."
—Debbie Dailey, university professor and parent

Perhaps this analogy clarifies. How do you keep your heart healthy? In addition to eating right, you must exercise aerobically—you need to give your cardiovascular system a workout complete with increased heart rate and intense breathing. You need to break a sweat. How do you keep your brain healthy? You need to break an "academic sweat" (Roberts & Inman, 2009, p. 10). To exercise the brain, it needs novelty, challenge, and complexity; it must think. When we leave gifted kids on their own to read, to do worksheets, etc., we do not encourage that deep thinking so necessary for growth. Educators must be the academic coaches who assess the strengths and skills of their academic athletes, then design rigorous workouts so they have continuous growth.

Grade skipping is socially and emotionally damaging.

Acceleration, the process in which students move at a faster pace through a specific content or grade level than age-based peers, may be one of the most misunderstood concepts in gifted education. According to NAGC leadership Tracy Cross and George Betts (2015), "Historically, the great paradox of acceleration has been that the beliefs and practices of educators (and the general public) did not align with the research evidence" (p. vii).

In 2004, the Templeton Foundation funded a meta-analysis (a synthesis of known research on a topic) on acceleration in its landmark study, *A Nation Deceived: How Schools Hold Back America's Brightest Students* (Colangelo, Assouline, & Gross, 2004). In short, the 50-plus years of compiled research argued that there was no more effective service for gifted students—and most cost effective for schools—than acceleration when properly administered. And, instead of being socially and emotionally damaging, appropriate acceleration provided the venue for healthy social and emotional development. The follow-up work, *A Nation Empowered: Evidence Trumps the Excuses Holding Back America's Brightest Students* (Assouline, Colangelo, VanTassel-Baska, & Lupkowski-Shoplik, 2015), not only added scholarly insight and research, but it also told the stories of those accelerated. Additionally, it listed 20 different types of acceleration from grade skipping to early entrance into kindergarten to curriculum compacting. (Chapter 5 explores these options and more.) Both volumes of these reports are available on the web (see For More Information at the end of this chapter). All parents, administrators, and educators of gifted children should read these critical works. As gifted education expert Jonathan Wai (2015) stated, "All students deserve to learn something new each day, and if academically talented students desire to be accelerated and are ready for it, the long-term evidence clearly supports the intervention" (p. 73).

Gifted kids are needed in every class to be role models.

An in-depth review of years of research completed on role modeling found that children tend to "pattern their behaviors after competent rather than incompetent peers" (Schunk, 1987, p. 167)—which could be one reason behind this myth. However, this research also indicated that children tend to model themselves after those who are similar in ability. In short, when great discrepancies are present, no modeling occurs because children cannot make connections between themselves and the model. This damaging myth provides some of the basis for the "sprinkle method" often used by principals when creating elementary classrooms: They sprinkle the gifted children, one or two to a room, in order to have strong academic and behavioral role models for others. Not only is this faulty thinking regarding role models, but it is also flawed in regard to what the children are modeling—not all gifted children are achievers nor are they ideal, well-behaved students.

Using gifted students as tutors is a good service for them.

All too often well-meaning educators pair the gifted child with the struggling child, as parent Claire Hughes related. She said one of her greatest challenges is "getting her daughter's teachers to do something with her beyond teach other kids." Educators get master's degrees in order to learn best practice and hone teaching skills, yet somehow they think something magical will occur when pairing the child who gets it with the child who doesn't. Research on motivating students (McCombs, 2010) tells us not to

> pair struggling students with students of higher ability or greater knowledge and skills, as this may result in students becoming dependent (rather than independent) learners. Unless high-ability students are trained to work as positive tutors,

motivation to learn can suffer (e.g., Harter, 2006; King, Staffieri, & Adelgais, 1998; O'Donnell, 1999). (p. 2)

The goal of learning is continuous for all learners, so we certainly don't want to do anything to discourage independent learning and motivation. STEM magnet school teacher Jennifer Sheffield argued:

> Gifted students are *not* tutors. I can't emphasize this enough. They deserve to be learning new things every day, just like any other student. It is not their responsibility to try to teach a classmate who is struggling with content. This puts both students in an awkward position and can be a very frustrating experience.

She explained that it is better to encourage the student to be "acknowledged as the class expert on a particular subject or a project assignment or to teach a lesson on a topic of interest in class one day." Having gifted kids tutor other students can be a disservice to all.

Gifted students are high achievers.

Students with intellectual gifts and talents have the potential to be high achieving; whether they are is more of a question of determination, work ethic, and grit than ability and potential. Students identified in creativity, leadership, or the visual and performing arts have the potential to excel in their areas of giftedness—yet their achievement may not be school-related at all. Too often people expect someone identified as gifted to be the straight-A student (in all areas, not just his area of giftedness—but that's another myth). Underachievement—where a student's performance does not match ability—runs rampant in gifted students. (See Chapter 6 for more discussion.) In fact, researchers have speculated that between 10–50% of gifted students are underachievers; the wide range stems from differing definitions of giftedness and underachievement (Siegle & McCoach, 2008). Gifted and talented resource teacher Angie Barrandeguy noted:

> In my experience, many teachers believe if a student is identified as gifted in an area that he or she should automatically excel in that subject area. Sometimes students are not motivated or

do not see the importance of repetition in homework and/or are not very well organized to turn in assignments. Although the students are gifted, these traits do not always make the best students.

IQ or achievement tests are effective ways to identify gifted students.

Tests and other measures can be wonderful tools that provide information about your child's ability or achievement levels, but they are simply tools. No one number defines a child. In fact, a child can take the same test several times, scoring differently each time. Was she sleepy? Did he have breakfast? Was the room too cold or hot? Did the child next to her click his pencil on the desk? So many factors—as well as ability or achievement level—affect test outcomes. Measurement error should be taken into account. A student who scores a 120 on the Wechsler Intelligence Scale for Children®–Fifth Edition (WISC®–V, 2014), a commonly used IQ assessment, may very well be gifted even though she doesn't hit the magical 130. That 120 score should only be one indicator. According to gifted education scholar Frank Worrell (2009), "It is clear that no single score allows us to make the most accurate predictions about outstanding performance, even in the academic domains . . . . Outstanding accomplishments by children and adults are *multivariate* in nature and require multivariate explanations" (p. 244). Best practice dictates multiple measures being used for identification in any of the five areas.

"If we allow ourselves to challenge, question, and probe some of gifted education's myths, we can develop new models and approaches that will be practical, cost-efficient, and readily implemented in schools." (Treffinger, 2009, p. 232)

A child with a learning difficulty cannot be gifted.

Students can have multiple exceptionalities: A child may be gifted in language arts but have bipolar disorder; she may be a gifted singer who is also blind; he may have an IQ of 150 accompanied by a reading disability—the list continues. These children often struggle in school. Often they are never identified as gifted because their other exceptionality masks their giftedness. Sometimes they are not identified through special education because they have developed effective coping skills to deal with the exceptionality. Or, as professor and scholar Sydney Moon (2009) stated, "Perhaps the most at-risk subpopulation of gifted students is the twice exceptional. These students face difficult problems and challenges throughout their schooling that make it difficult for them to be successful academically, much less to fully develop their talents" (p. 275). (Chapter 9 explores twice-exceptional children.)

Final Thoughts

From all children being gifted to no students with disabilities being gifted, myths surrounding gifted learners thrive in our schools and communities. Unfortunately, well-meaning educators, school board members, and other decision makers believe these myths and base curriculum choices, school policy, and even state legislation on erroneous —and even harmful—information. Parents also buy into the mythology, unknowingly letting inaccuracies cloud their decisions regarding home and school for their child. Imagine what could happen if these myths were systemically debunked!

Implications for Home

+ How do these myths play into your life at home? First, honestly question your own beliefs and debunk the myths that you hold to be truths. Then share the myths with family and friends who interact with your child.
+ Have realistic expectations for your child, especially if your child is twice exceptional. You may need to raise expectations or lower them.
+ If you suspect underachievement, skip to Chapter 6.

+ Listen and be understanding about the challenges and frustrations in school.
+ Depending on the challenge level or perceived importance of it, homework may be an issue. Discover where the real issues lie: Is it too much repetition? Does your child consider it busywork? Have the facts before you intervene. It's vitally important to voice support of teachers and school to your child (more on that in Chapter 7).
+ Encourage your child to have idea-mates not just age-mates.

Implications for School

+ Remember the importance of open communication with your child's school. Share the myths with your child's educators. Educated, well-meaning professionals may have gaps in their knowledge, especially in regard to gifted education. Most educators have never had an undergraduate college class on gifted education; some may have covered one chapter on it—if the professor didn't omit it. Many have not had professional development in gifted education either.
+ Provide resources if possible. For example, share the website for the acceleration studies.

For More Information

+ *A Nation Deceived: How Schools Hold Back America's Brightest Students* by Nicholas Colangelo, Susan G. Assouline, and Miraca U. M. Gross (The University of Iowa, The Connie Belin & Jacqueline N. Blank International Center for Gifted Education and Talent Development, 2004)—This 2004 watershed report can be downloaded at http://www.acceleration institute.org.
+ *A Nation Empowered: Evidence Trumps the Excuses Holding Back America's Brightest Students* by Susan G. Assouline, Nicholas Colangelo, Joyce VanTassel-Baska, and Ann Lupkowski-

Shoplik (The University of Iowa, The Connie Belin & Jacqueline N. Blank International Center for Gifted Education and Talent Development, 2015)—The follow-up to *A Nation Deceived*, this report can be purchased at http://www.accelerationinstitute.org.

+ "Myriad Myths About Giftedness" by Duke TIP (2010)— This discussion on myths about giftedness is available on the Duke TIP website at http://tip.duke.edu/node/934.

+ "Myths About Gifted Students" by NAGC (n.d.)—NAGC also explores the myths permeating gifted education at https://www.nagc.org/resources-publications/resources/myths-about-gifted-students.

+ "Demythologizing Gifted Education," a special issue of *Gifted Child Quarterly* edited by Don Treffinger and Carolyn Callahan (2009; 53 [4])—One of the leading journals in gifted education devoted an entire issue to gifted myths. If you are a member of NAGC, visit http://gcq.sagepub.com/content/53/4.toc for more information. As a member, you can also listen to a podcast with the editors at http://gcq.sagepub.com/content/suppl/2009/09/21/53.4.DC1.

+ "Demythologizing Gifted Education: A 25-Year Journey" by Donald Treffinger—Guest editor Don Treffinger gave an overview of the myths in *Teaching for High Potential* (also available to NAGC members only—which is a great reason to join) at http://www.nagc.org.442elmp01.blackmesh.com/sites/default/files/files/resource/Bridging_the_Divide.pdf.

+ "Top 10 Myths in Gifted Education" by Gifted and Talented Association of Montgomery County (2010)—Baltimore public school students created this video available on YouTube at https://www.youtube.com/watch?v=MDJst-y_ptI.

chapter 3

What Does a Gifted Child Look Like?

Bright children are often opinionated and can be quite obstinate. They are often hard to parent as they are quite stubborn and also can be quite self-sufficient. Don't let this fool you; they definitely need boundaries and parenting. They doubt themselves and lack self-confidence just like most children. All children need love and reassurance even when they think they are—and sometimes are—smarter than their parents.

—Karen Bickett, parent

Cognitive Characteristics: How Gifted Children Think and Learn

As discussed in Chapter 2, it is important to note that all children are different. Although characteristics will vary based on individual personalities and areas of giftedness, there are some general characteristics of gifted children. Many of these traits are common in all children, but gifted kids often have a "greater dose" of these attributes (Duke TIP, 2012a). The following cognitive characteristics of gifted children can be found in almost any resource on the gifted, but here are a few of the ones we used in this book:

+ "Common Characteristics of Gifted Individuals" by NAGC (https://www.nagc.org/resources-publications/resources/my-child-gifted/common-characteristics-gifted-individuals);

 DOI: 10.4324/9781003237013-4

+ *A Parent's Guide to Gifted Children* by Jim Webb, Janet Gore, Ed Amend, and Arlene DeVries (Great Potential Press, 2007); and
+ *The Survival Guide for Parents of Gifted Kids* by Sally Walker (Free Spirit, 2002).

Gifted kids are inquisitive and observant.

"How does that work?" "Why did that happen?" "What would happen if . . . ?" Chances are you have heard these same questions from your child—the how and why type of questions that gifted children often ask. They are fascinated with the world around them and have an intense curiosity about how things work. Gifted children are often more observant than their age-mates; for instance, they may pick up on the fact that a teacher looks stressed after a morning meeting or that Mom seems in a happy mood today because she was humming in the car while she drank her coffee.

They like to know and understand what is going on and to be well informed about events at home, at school, or often national and world events. When the adults are talking in the next room, they may ask questions about the conversation just to make sure they aren't left out of the "family" discussion. They may continually ask probing questions and may challenge facts so they can understand the hows and whys behind those facts. On a family road trip, for example, questions about how roads were built, who built them, who made the road signs, why they are green, how people know how much gas their cars use, and so on, show their need to understand and make meaning of the world around them.

Jane Paulin, teacher, described this inquisitive nature:

I think a gifted student will make connections between content areas, between what's being learned and other things they have done, read, or seen. They see things differently than most others. They are interested in things when you can't understand what causes their interest—I knew a 2-year-old who would constantly ask "What time is it?"

Teacher Jennifer Sheffield stated, "Gifted students often ask seemingly off-the-wall questions. They frequently have a very deep and/or broad understanding of topics of interest and quickly make connections." Because of their inquisitive nature, gifted children may question parents, teachers, coaches, or other authority figures and want to share their own opinions and experiences on topics; this questioning isn't always appreciated by these adults, who may see it more as defiance than curiosity. Andrew McMichael, parent of gifted children, mentioned his concern for his sons' many questions as a "constant worry that the curiosity won't kill the cat." Some gifted children may even struggle with relaxing or resting because their minds are thinking of many things at the same time. A gifted preschooler once argued to avoid naptime: "Mom, I can't rest. There are just so many things in the world to think about."

Gifted kids process information quickly and remember details longer than their same-age peers.

Picture this conversation with a distraught fifth grader: "Mom, do you remember that play in first grade that you missed because of work, and I wore a green shirt, and Ms. Smith made us all sit on the bleachers with our drinks? Well, it was a good play, but this year's isn't going to be because nobody knows the lines." Imagine a third-grade boy who can quote team wins, losses, and most valuable players from the last several weeks of NFL football play. These might be similar to conversations you have had with your child because gifted children usually have an excellent ability to remember facts and details. Because of this ability, they can process new content or new learning much faster than the average student, making connections between the old and new. They do not need lengthy repetition or practice to learn vocabulary words, science concepts, or parts of speech, for example. They may become bored and impatient when they have to define words they already know, work 20 math problems when they know how to do it after the first two, re-read books or stories, or complete review sheets answering the same questions again. In fact, "gifted students often refuse to do work they consider meaningless or rote" (Jennifer Sheffield, gifted teacher). They are used to answering questions in class and often getting the answer right. Because remembering comes easily for them, they may hate to be wrong, to miss points on assignments, or to take constructive criticism.

Over the last several years, brain researchers have studied various physical attributes of the gifted brain that impact information processing and learning. While numerous books and articles have been written explaining the complex functioning of the brain, a few generalizations describe the key findings. Because of differences in the gifted brain, a gifted child can pay closer attention to events and stimuli, can absorb and process that information at a much faster pace than his or her same-age peers, can stay focused longer, can make connections between ideas and events, and can remember things longer. In *Enriching the Brain: How to Maximize Every Learner's Potential* (2006), brain researcher and author Eric Jensen explained how the gifted brain processes information using this fascinating analogy about technology:

> For comparison, think about all the technology that surrounds you right now. You needn't be deeply into the high-tech life to have a computer or two in the house, along with several phones of various types, a few TV sets (probably with DVD player and VCR), TIVO, Internet access, videogames, an iPod, and any number of other devices, from a PDA to a talking oven. Could you imagine the work in networking together all those devices in just one house, your own? This would mean a complete wireless network within your house. Let's say you did have the savvy to interface all your different types of systems into one streaming, trouble-free, seamless network. That would be tricky, but it could be done. Now add this: next you're making every bit of technology in your home talk to every bit of technology in someone's home down the street. Now add this: you're making every bit of technology in your home talk to one in three homes around the world. You've just bumped your home-networking problem into a global challenge of near-biblical proportions. If that sounds complex, that's the equivalent of what every human brain does! The gifted brain simply does it all quicker. (pp. 157–158)

For detailed information on how the gifted brain functions, see the list of recommended books at the end of this chapter.

Gifted kids are abstract, conceptual thinkers and problem solvers.
"What if we tried to solve the math problem without those steps?"
"Why is a story about a spider spinning words into a web such a famous book that everyone reads?" "What if we build the bridge out of pretzels instead of toothpicks?" These questions show how gifted children are capable of complex, abstract thinking about a variety of topics. Because they usually learn facts at a faster pace than their peers, they are ready to apply their knowledge, figure out how to solve problems with a variety of variables, and analytically think about characters or plot lines in a story. They are able to grasp big ideas and connections between content areas, such as how math impacts the world of science or how literary characters fit into a historical time period.

Gifted children "ask questions that reflect the big picture and think in concepts more than with details," stated Cecelia Boswell, former building principal and district administrator. She further explained, "Gifted children have the ability to take new information and create a new way of looking at it, to think about the 'what ifs' with the new information." Amy Berry, parent, described her son's conceptual thinking in math:

> He sees patterns so quickly. Some of my parent friends had complained about the new math techniques being taught and how confusing it can be to help kids with homework. I brought up the subject with my son, specifically mentioning multiplying with the lattice technique (which was completely foreign to me). He was totally unfazed and told me, "I can show you."

Gifted kids may have an intensity or passion about a topic of interest.
Imagine an 8-year-old boy who is so fascinated with dinosaurs that he has read all the books in the school and town libraries, spent hours perusing websites on dinosaurs, created sketches of his favorite dinosaurs in art class, and asked to purchase dinosaur-shaped chicken nuggets at the grocery (only to be disappointed when realizing they do not accurately depict any of the dinosaurs he has been studying). Having a passion and intensity for learning, and maybe even particular topics, is

a trait of gifted children. They often can stay focused for many hours, even at a young age, when learning about the subjects they love.

"We have to help gifted students find their passions and provide a safety net for those occasions when we want to stretch them a bit. We must gauge our gifted students' skills and abilities, so we can provide them with rich opportunities for continued growth. Learning about our students is a critical component of our job but so is helping our students learn about themselves."

—David Baxter, parent and elementary teacher

Gifted kids are usually creative thinkers with novel approaches to solving problems.

"Dad, what if the leaf blower had a different component on the side like this one in my drawing? I think that would make the whole process of clearing leaves much more efficient," said a gifted first grader, sitting in the floor of the garage coloring and watching Dad do the yard work. Such creative thinking and vivid imaginations are characteristics of gifted kids. They often can think of better ways of solving a problem and can create diagrams or ideas for new inventions. In school, they can usually demonstrate their knowledge in a variety of ways, using a variety of products.

Gifted kids are usually effective communicators.

"I had a conflict this morning because my shoes didn't match my shirt, and my favorite shirt was in the laundry. This is totally unacceptable to my sense of fashion," explained a gifted 3-year-old to her preschool teacher. *Conflict? Unacceptable? Sense of fashion?* These are advanced vocabulary words and concepts for a 3-year-old. Most gifted children are very verbal, with an advanced vocabulary compared to other same-age peers. Often, gifted kids will speak and read earlier than their peers and will ask questions about words they don't know or events they don't understand. Some gifted students are avid readers, with a book in their hands during every spare minute of the day. They are usually capable of having in-depth conversations about characters in books or movies, motives behind their actions, and how events in the plot might have turned out differently.

Gifted kids usually have an advanced sense of humor.

Gifted kids tend to enjoy jokes, word games, cartoons, and sarcasm because they understand the vocabulary, irony, or play on words that makes the jokes or cartoons funny. Dina Chaffin, district coordinator, observed this about gifted children's senses of humor:

> Years ago we used a video series to supplement our third-grade science curriculum called *Science Court*. *Science Court* had quite a bit of humor in it that 95% of the kids didn't get, but gifted kids always got the jokes and laughed. Since my third graders weren't formally identified, I would note the names of the students that got the jokes on *Science Court* and then check to see who was on the G/T list when it came out the next year. Every child that caught the humor would be on the G/T list!

After learning about characteristics of gifted students in a teacher education university class, Zach Johnson, an aspiring teacher, who was in gifted programs throughout school, reflected:

> That makes so much sense. I always knew I was funny, but I could never understand why kids in my classes didn't laugh at my jokes. It took until middle school or high school for them to laugh with me and validate that I was funny.

Gifted kids often exhibit sensitivity and strong emotions.

"Ms. Lee, I brought you a cookie from the cafeteria and drew you a picture because this morning when you were taking attendance, you looked very sad at your computer." "Mom, I'm so mad because in our school Thanksgiving play, all the kids playing the Pilgrims are not taking it seriously, and we are going to look bad in front of all the parents." Such comments by gifted kids show a strong sensitivity to others' emotions and strong feelings about events that happen at school or home. At times, it may be hard for a gifted child to understand why her same-age peers are not as upset about what happened in play practice as she is; at other times, however, gifted kids can be intuitive and empathize with others' feelings and moods.

Gifted kids often have a heightened sense of justice and a need for fairness.

"Mom, can you explain to me the difference in Republicans and Democrats, and why everyone seems so upset about this election? Can't they all just get along and try to make the country better?" asked a gifted 6-year-old on her ride home from school because she didn't understand the politicians' radio ads during election season. This awareness of social issues and a desire for justice and fair play are traits of gifted kids. Gary Davis, Sylvia Rimm, and Del Siegle (2011) said that gifted children are "likely to develop, refine, and internalize a system of values and a keen sense of fair play and justice at a relatively early age" (p. 40). Because of their inquisitive nature and acute observation skills, they are often aware of complex social issues or problems much earlier than their peers. As they grapple with abstract notions like freedom, justice, and equality, it is often hard for them to understand when people aren't treated fairly or adults don't live by the rules of right and wrong. Similarly, classroom situations in which a whole class loses recess when only part of the class didn't complete their work may trigger their desire to argue for fairness in a letter to the principal. Kandy Smith, parent and former elementary school principal, described, "Many gifted children have a heightened sense of fairness—one of the hardest things to circumvent as almost nothing seems fair to a very young child . . . or even to adults."

"I think everyone would benefit from understanding more about gifted children's special needs. So many people think of high achievers and autonomous learners when they think of gifted children. They don't really understand the intensity and sensitivities that come along with high intellectual ability. When leaders see gifted students from a special educational perspective, when they see the vulnerabilities of these children, they are more likely to support programming for gifted children."
—Lynette Breedlove, administrator

Gifted kids often have a strong sense of self and a sense of responsibility.

"Grandma, let's check to see if we have everything before we go to the mall. Do you have your purse? Do you have your keys? Do you have me?" These are examples of questions from a 3-year-old gifted child before an outing with his favorite babysitter, his grandmother. Spoken like a child much older than 3, his sense of responsibility to take care of things was evident, even at a very young age. Gifted kids often have a well-developed awareness of themselves and their environment. This can lead to a strong sense of responsibility; gifted students are often chosen as leaders for class projects, helpers for substitutes, or members of a principal's student advisory committee. They often have a strong desire to help others in their home and school environments. Constance Baynum, teacher, described such a student:

> A second grader saw an old microscope retired on a ledge in our gifted area. He said, "Mrs. Baynum, someday could I see that microscope? I asked for one for Christmas, but it cost too much." Two weeks later, this gifted young boy brought his rock collection and taught an interesting 20-minute session on rocks as seen under a microscope. Everyone left, and he came running back and hugged me. "I'm so happy I used a microscope. Someday I'm going to use a microscope to find a cure for cancer! Did you know animals get cancer too?"

Gifted kids may be perfectionists.

"Okay. So here is how I see it. We have to sell the most popcorn and icees tonight in order to make the most profit and be the winners. Here is the best plan for how to make that work perfectly," said a fifth-grade gifted student at her school's Entrepreneur Fair. Was she correct? Probably. Was her plan what her partners wanted to accomplish? Maybe not. Gifted children can set very high, sometimes even unrealistic, expectations for themselves, perhaps getting upset when making a 98 on a test instead of a 100. Jennifer Sheffield, educator, described gifted children as "often highly critical with a fear of failure." For more information on perfectionism, see Chapter 4.

Final Thoughts

Each gifted child is unique. It is important to remember that gifted children may not exhibit all of the characteristics above, or they may display different traits at different times. All children are different, and each gifted child has a unique combination of personality traits and areas of giftedness. Teacher Jane Paulin described this diversity:

> They're different from high achievers. They may be low achievers. They may act out because they don't know what to do with all the ideas running through their heads. They may be socially awkward. Of course, they may also be high achievers, well-behaved, and socially adept. There isn't a box.

It is also important to remember that each of the traits above can manifest itself in both positive and negative ways. Being organized and goal-oriented is a positive trait when working on a project alone, but it may cause other students in the group project not to have a say in how the work is done. Wanting to ask questions in order to understand how things work or why rules exist may be appropriate at times, but at other times it's important to follow a rule obediently and efficiently.

Another significant variable in describing characteristics of gifted kids is that development is sometimes asynchronous. This means that one aspect of the child—such as his cognitive ability—develops much faster than another aspect—such as his fine motor skills. A sixth-grade student who is capable of talking about ways to deal with world hunger and how he can play a role in that story on one day may cry and slam the door of his room over an argument with his sister about the television remote the next day. One parent (Anonymous, 2007) described asynchronous development this way:

> Alex is clearly gifted when observed through one lens and yet obviously lagging when viewed from a different angle. He knew his letters at 20 months but didn't learn to tie his shoes until the middle of second grade. He taught himself to read just before his third birthday, but in third grade he still doesn't have any

close friends. He reveled in his discovery of factorials shortly after he turned 5, yet stubbing his toe can trigger an hours-long meltdown even as he approaches his 9th birthday. (p. 20)

As parents it is important to know your child's specific gifted characteristics in order to understand how they may impact her life at home and at school.

Implications for Home

How do the traits of gifted children impact life at home and parenting roles and responsibilities? Kandy Smith, parent and former elementary school principal, summarized the challenge of parenting gifted children at home and school as follows:

Listen. Your children will tell you what they need. They will let you know what feels good to them and what they fear. Know that the brainpower a child has is not the child—only a component of who he is. The affective aspects of growing a quality human being include far more than just academic success. Not only is your child likely the "smartest one in the room" most of the time, but he KNOWS he is the smartest one in the room. It is not always easy to tone that knowledge down while keeping her on her toes as risk takers. Childrearing is not easy in the best of circumstances. It is hard to listen to what is said, what is meant, what is missing that needed to be said, and what is really being felt. And that entire combination changes every day—sometimes every hour and will likely never stop. It is not easy to feed the fire in a child while constantly trying to keep the fire under control, but the joys are many and sweet.

While every child is an individual with unique gifts and personalities, here are some general parenting tips for both home and school to help "feed the fire" in your gifted child:

+ For the gifted child who is inquisitive and constantly asking questions, collect resource books such as fact books, almanacs, atlases, a collection of suitable websites, online encyclopedias, a thesaurus, or a magazine subscription on her topic of interest. Find peers or groups who share similar interests, whether that interest is soccer, astronomy, or acting. Seek out programs at local universities or libraries on your child's favorite topics (Walker, 2002). Elementary teacher Deborah Strubler said, "If he is not interested in baseball, do not buy the $300 bat and force the issue. Take him to the rock and mineral show and buy him the $300 arrowhead from the Paleo period if that is his love!"

+ Because gifted children are often very verbal at a young age and can have conversations about complex topics, it is important to make time to talk to your child every day. Debrief her experiences in school each day at dinner, talk about your day's highs and lows before bed each night, or ask questions during rides to and from school each day. Keep her talking about what she enjoys in her day and what her concerns or challenges are.

+ Because of their ability to have adult conversations often beyond their age or years of experience, sometimes it's easy to forget that they are just children. Allow them freedoms or responsibilities that are appropriate for their emotional or social development. For instance, don't allow unlimited choices for what to do on a free Saturday; rather, narrow the options and let the child choose to either visit the zoo or see a play.

+ For the child who tends to be a perfectionist, show him that it is okay to make mistakes. Share examples from your job or events in your day about how you first didn't understand something, then figured it out. Model how you learn and try new things that sometimes work and sometimes don't. Be sure to talk about what you learned and how you will apply that lesson in your life.

+ For the child who is empathetic and very sensitive of social issues and fairness, make sure to model good behavior and respect of others. Highly observant gifted kids notice when an adult's words and actions don't match. Model respect and respectful talk about school, family members, sports officials, and work colleagues. Sylvia Rimm, author of *How to Parent So*

Children Will Learn: Top Ten List (2010), stated the importance of being a role model:

> Be a role model of ethics, activity, and hard work. Locate other good role models for your children. Your children are watching you. When you "get away with" speeding, keep too much change, or are disrespectful to your parents (their grandparents), they'll notice. When you're interesting and energetic they'll be equally impressed. You can be a good role model without being perfect, but your imperfections are showing. You don't have to do it all. Introduce your children to friends and potential mentors who also will be positive influences. (para. 9)

✝   For the gifted child who demonstrates a heightened sense of justice and empathy for social concerns, find opportunities for her to participate in acts of service that can make a difference. Find volunteer opportunities at the Salvation Army or another nonprofit that interests your child. Collect money to shop for a child or family at Christmas. Buy food for a local food pantry.

Remember that for each of the gifted traits listed, there are positive and negative manifestations of them. For instance, the child with a passion for dinosaurs may be able to spend hours reading books on that topic but may quickly tire of working math problems in class. The gifted child who is a perfectionist may always bring home an A on his report card but may be frustrated when a task is too hard to master quickly. The curious, inquisitive child may be fascinated and want to ask continuous questions about every topic but may have trouble listening and focusing in class while a story is being read or accepting the rules for recess when a teacher explains them to the class.

As parents, the challenge is to help hone the positive manifestations of traits and help children learn to manage the negative manifestations of gifted traits. Remember that in most instances, these traits are how the child is "hardwired" to think and learn; they aren't a choice. Explain when it is appropriate to debate, argue, or ask questions and when and how an authority figure must be respected and not questioned. Explain when it is okay to blurt out questions and when to listen. Remember that their traits may be asynchronous, occurring in stages and at different times. Be patient and understanding with your child as these learning and socialization processes occur.

Implications for School

Gifted children's characteristics can create great successes and sometimes frustrating challenges for your child in the school setting. Chapter 1 discussed the myths of giftedness, and these myths can sometimes affect the experiences gifted children have in school. Joan Smutny, author of "Characteristics and Development" in *Parenting Gifted Children* (2011a), discussed the impact of these stereotypes in school:

> The stereotype of giftedness—what it looks like and how it appears in the classroom—is still so strong that even the keenest observers tend to equate giftedness with achievement. But parents see much more in their children—the exceptional ability, yes, but also their heightened sensitivities, intuitive understanding, empathy far beyond their years; also their untraditional ways of learning. Taken together, these characteristics can present special challenges in school. (p. 37)

Understanding your child and being an advocate for her with teachers at school is extremely important, as expressed by Ruth Kertis, resource teacher:

> I would like classroom teachers to be more familiar with the characteristics of gifted students. For example, gifted students are not always the highest performing students in the class. They are sometimes the students who are unorganized, do not complete class work, and are sometimes distracted or not paying

attention to instruction. They also may be the students who have anxiety because they want everything they do to be perfect.

You know your child better than anyone else. You understand your child's unique personality, gifted traits, interest areas, and learning needs. Be an advocate for your child and a partner to your child's teachers. The following tips are general recommendations and strategies for helping your child be successful in school:

+   Be informed of challenges that your child's cognitive traits may pose in the classroom. What happens if she has already read *Charlotte's Web,* and the fourth-grade class is reading that book? What if he can already read when starting kindergarten, and class begins with learning numbers and letters in the month of August? How accepting is the teacher of a barrage of questions? Is there a time during the week when students share their interests?

+   Be aware of whether or not your child is mastering concepts quicker than peers. Talk to your child and the teacher. If she has mastered the concepts and skills, what is she learning and how is she being challenged? How is the teacher providing continuous progress in learning for your child?

+   Be open and encouraging for your student to take risks and learn new skills, even if they are hard and may be a struggle. Talk to him about making mistakes and learning from them. Parent Karen Bickett stated:

> My most trying moments as a parent have been when my children have doubted themselves and their abilities. It is always hard to watch a child struggle, but it is a very important part of growing up. All children should be allowed to fail and have to develop the resilience to persevere. A gifted child that has not learned humility is not only unpleasant to be around socially, but they are also less likely to embrace challenging situations.

+ Most importantly, be ready to communicate with your child's teachers, curriculum coordinator, and administrators if needed.

For More Information

+ "Cognitive Characteristics of Gifted Students: Smooth Sailing, Rough Seas" by Duke TIP (2012)—This video, available at https://vimeo.com/41713778, provides an overview of cognitive traits of gifted kids.
+ "Dr. Sylvia Rimm's Articles for Parents and Teachers"—Sylvia Rimm's website includes a collection of helpful articles for parents and teachers at http://www.sylviarimm.com/parentingarticles.html.
+ *Dr. Sylvia Rimm's Smart Parenting: How to Raise a Happy, Achieving Child* by Sylvia Rimm (Crown, 1996): Rimm's book is a great resource containing numerous strategies for successful parenting.
+ *How the Gifted Brain Learns* by David Sousa (Corwin, 2009)—Sousa's book is an interesting read for information on how a gifted child's brain functions.
+ *Enriching the Brain: How to Maximize Every Learner's Potential* by Eric Jensen (Jossey-Bass, 2009)—This is a wonderful resource for understanding how the brain works and how brain research affects learning in schools.

chapter 4

What Are the Social and Emotional Needs of Gifted Children?

An enhanced capacity for feeling is essential to the production of great art, moving music, high drama, memorable prose and poetry, and exquisite performances. We love to watch the ecstatic absorption of a conductor, the passionate portrayal of Othello, and the dedicated delicacy of a ballerina.
—Linda Silverman, psychologist

Just as gifted children have unique cognitive characteristics, they also have unique social and emotional traits. What do we mean by social and emotional traits? Duke TIP's *Social and Emotional Characteristics: Rough Sailing, Smooth Seas* video (2012b) defined social traits as those related to interpersonal awareness, such as the "ability to read social situations, recognize body language and facial expressions, and interpret the emotions of others." Social traits can be observed as children interact with peers and adults, in class and club leadership roles, or in interactions within the family. Emotional traits are related to intrapersonal awareness, such as the "capacity to recognize one's own emotions, motivations, and needs" (Duke TIP, 2012b).

Emotional traits can be demonstrated through an individual's level of self-esteem, his motivation to learn, or the ability to persevere in difficult tasks. As we discuss typical social and emotional characteristics of gifted children, it is critical to remember that each child is unique, with varying personalities, gifts, talents, and dispositions. *The Social and Emotional Development of Gifted Children* (Robinson, Reis, Neihart, & Moon, 2002) described this diversity as follows:

DOI: 10.4324/9781003237013-5

There is no more varied group of young people than the diverse group known as gifted children and adolescents. Not only do they come from every walk of life, every ethnic and socioeconomic group, and every nation, but they also exhibit an almost unlimited range of personal characteristics in temperament, risk taking, and conservatism, introversion and extroversion, reticence and assertiveness, and degree of effort in reaching goals. Furthermore, no standard pattern of talent exists among gifted individuals. Included in this group are both those moderately advanced students who might be overlooked in a regular classroom setting and those whose talents are so far from the usual range that they have an obvious need for dramatic educational adjustments. (p. xi)

While the social and emotional traits discussed below are in and of themselves neutral, the behaviors that sometimes manifest themselves with these traits in social settings may be perceived as positive or negative by both peers and adults.

Intensity

Gifted students often exhibit a heightened intensity in how they experience and interact with the world around them; this intensity often begins at a very young age, as expressed by this mother's (Leslie Hutchinson), description of her daughter's early years:

My daughter has always behaved very well in school (hello, perfectionism), but at home she has been a real challenge. Even her first night home from the hospital we knew we were in for more than we bargained. She seemed to need more . . . more of everything . . . constant breastfeeding or pacifier use, constant touch, constant change of scenery. I didn't know a baby could be bored. But she was! And bored quickly! I had to keep her bouncing, moving, and sucking on something ALL THE TIME. One thing she did seem to need less of was sleep. I couldn't understand how she could function on such a small amount of sleep. She still does as a preteen.

In "Emotional Intensity in Gifted Children" (n.d.), Lesley Sword described intensity in gifted children this way:

> Just as gifted children's thinking is more complex and has more depth than other children's, so too are their emotions more complex and more intense. Complexity can be seen in the vast range of emotions that gifted children can experience at any one time and the intensity is evident in the "full-on-ness" about everything with which parents and teachers of the gifted children are so familiar. Emotional intensity in the gifted is not a matter of feeling more than the other people, but a different way of experiencing the world: vivid, absorbing, penetrating, encompassing, complex, commanding—a way of being quiveringly alive. (p. 1)

In gifted children, this intensity, this experiencing of the world in a different way, can be expressed in both positive and negative ways, depending on the unique personality and disposition of the child. One expression of intense reactions could be in bodily symptoms such as feeling nervous with an upset stomach or feeling shy and physically blushing. Imagine the first-grade gifted student who has a stomach ache for the first part of the school year because of a concern to do well and meet the teacher's expectations. This intensity often manifests itself in strong emotional attachments to others, as in the kindergartner who sobbed because the year was over and "there will NEVER be another teacher who understands her like Ms. Newcomb."

Another manifestation of intensity could be in fear or anxiety with an exaggerated sense of worry in response to a social problem or situation. For instance, after seeing a video on homeless children in a crowded large city, a gifted 7-year-old might feel guilty or worried about eating too much at dinner or at a birthday party. Gifted researchers Nancy Robinson, Sally Reis, Maureen Neihart, and Sidney Moon (2002) explained these social worries or concerns:

Gifted children often have fears like those of older non-gifted children (for example, they encounter the dangers of nuclear warfare or the implications of the concept of infinity at an early age), but do not have the emotional control to put these insights aside and go on with their lives. Adults often expect gifted children to behave in all ways like older children and are confused and frustrated when the children prove unexpectedly "immature" by these exaggerated expectations. (pp. xvii–xviii)

As a parent, it is helpful to understand that the intensity or "full-on-ness" your child may exhibit as he encounters the world is normal and part of what makes him gifted. Some gifted psychologists and researchers refer to this intensity as an overexcitability (OE) and classify these OEs into five different categories.

"Parenting gifted children can be exhilarating and exhausting. Because they are so intellectually capable, it can be easy to assume that they also have the maturity that comes with knowledge. This is developmentally not the case. I had to remind myself many times that my children were in fact children and not mini adults. They mostly needed me to provide unconditional love in a world that was constantly judging and expecting so much of them. While I provided advocacy, enrichment opportunities, and a sounding board, I think in the end the most important thing I gave them was my acceptance."
—Tracy Harkins, parent

Overexcitabilities

Gifted expert Michael Piechowski (1991) described an overexcitability as "the great depth and intensity of emotional life expressed through a wide range of feelings, attachments, compassion, heightened sense of responsibility, and scrupulous self-examination" (p. 287).

Psychologist Kazimierz Dabrowski (as cited in Lind, 2001) explained OEs as "inborn intensities indicating a heightened ability to respond to stimuli" (p. 3). The following five OEs may be found in gifted children to varying degrees.

1. Psychomotor—the ability to be constantly on the move; full of energy; may need constant physical activity; highly competitive; rapid speech and gestures
2. Sensual—a heightened awareness to the experiences of sight, smell, touch, taste, and hearing; can be overstimulated or feel overwhelmed by too much noise, too many things to look at, or strong smells
3. Intellectual—a desire to understand how things are made, why things happen, how to solve the problem, or how parts fit together to make a whole; may be able to focus for long periods of item, especially on a topic of interest
4. Imaginational—a heightened sense of imagination and creativity; may doodle or daydream; may create stories or elaborate adventures
5. Emotional—the ability to experience strong and complex emotions; capable of compassion and empathy for others

Implications for Home

+ Honor a child's sensitivity to others and her environment. Accept and nurture without minimizing your child's emotions and intensity for his passion areas; help promote self-acceptance of these traits. Psychologists Martin Seligman and Mihaly Csikszentmihalyi (as cited in VanTassel-Baska, Cross, Olenchak, 2009) emphasized:

> Raising children . . . is vastly more than fixing what is wrong with them. It is about identifying and nurturing their strongest qualities, what they own and are best at, and helping them find niches in which they can best live out these strengths . . . . (p. 41)

+ Encourage your child to discuss both her positive and negative feelings openly. Sword (n.d.) suggested having your child use an emotional thermometer; for example, on a scale of 1–10, how are you feeling today? Help her to identify triggers of emotional responses in order to cope effectively with situations that create a nervous stomach or anxiety. Teach him awareness of his own behaviors and the effects those behaviors may have on others. Show her acceptable strategies for expressing or releasing her emotions such as listening to music, drawing, walking outside, or journaling.

+ Have clear and consistent behavioral expectations and enforce those with your child. Make sure your child knows that there are appropriate times and places to express emotions. It is not appropriate, for instance, to have a temper tantrum because a game with a sibling did not turn out as planned. For a child that exhibits intellectual OE, it is critical that he understands that some safety rules such as not walking into the street or not touching a hot stove must be obeyed without question.

+ Provide opportunities for expression each day. Allow children with psychomotor OEs time to have physical activity or unlimited talk time when it won't be a distraction to others around them. For sensual OEs, provide a quiet place to relax or listen to music somewhere in the house. Teach children with intellectual OEs how to solve problems in a way that respects others' opinions; model problem-solving strategies for them and share your successes and challenges in this area. For imaginational OEs, provide opportunities for creative play or let them help you develop solutions for challenges at home, such as making the best use of space in the garage.

Implications for School

+ If your child feels overwhelmed by a project or assignment, help her develop strategies for setting goals and developing a work plan. Help your child think through these questions: What does it take to get this task or project done? How can you best use your time to make that happen? What is a timeline to make it work? Help your child break down long-term projects into small, manageable tasks by setting realistic goals.

+ When your child has strong emotional reactions to events in school, find ways to help him calm down and cope with the emotions. Encourage a discussion of the emotions and the triggers, then figure out what destressors are for her. Jill Adelson and Hope Wilson, authors of *Letting Go of Perfect: Overcoming Perfectionism in Kids* (2009), suggested picking a calm time to talk to your child, such as on a car ride, while waiting in line, or during dinner. Allow your child to guide the conversation to help validate his feelings. Psychologist Linda Silverman (n.d.) stated:

> The first message an infant often hears is, "Hush, now, don't cry." And this message is reiterated throughout childhood—particularly to boys. The main lesson students learn in school is how to control, repress, deny their emotions, as part of the socialization process. (p. 1)

+ While it is important that children learn socially acceptable ways to express emotions, it is also critical to validate your child's feelings and not minimize them.

+ Communicate with your child's teacher his specific social and emotional needs. Share with the teacher what you have learned about her triggers and destressors. Encourage the teacher to possibly allow choices of assignments or products as much as possible. Help teachers to recognize that gifted and talented looks different with every student, as expressed by parent Leslie Hutchinson:

> Some teachers truly "got" her. Her third-grade teacher let her develop her own projects and present them at school. She happily grew butterflies from caterpillars at home and made a PowerPoint for her class. The teacher saw her strengths and let her run with them.

My daughter looks back at that year as the year she really got to learn in elementary school.

Perfectionism

In addition to intensity, some gifted children have perfectionist tendencies that can have implications for both home and school. Just like the characteristic of intensity, perfectionism as a trait can manifest itself in both positive and negative ways. Jill Adelson and Hope Wilson (2009) described two types of perfectionism—healthy and unhealthy. Healthy perfectionism allows children to set challenging yet realistic goals, to work toward mastery, and to earn a sense of pride as they strive for success through hard work. Unhealthy perfectionism can cause children to be overly competitive and focus on winning. It can lead to unrealistic goals that are often unattainable or impractical and to a low self-esteem and frustration. Jill Adelson (2007) further described types of perfectionist profiles: the Academic Achievers who must achieve a perfect score; the Aggravated Accuracy Assessors who are focused on being exact and redoing a project until it is perfect; the Risk Evaders who want to achieve all or nothing; the Controlling Image Managers who want to save face and manage their losses, adopting an "I could have if I wanted to" attitude; and the Procrastinating Perfectionists who often don't start a project until it is perfect in their mind in order to avoid failure. For more information on these types of perfectionism, check out the sources at the end of this chapter.

Implications for Home

+ Discuss with your child the difference between healthy and unhealthy perfectionism. Find teachable moments in your own life. Share how you worked hard to achieve personal or professional goals. Talk about mistakes you make and how you learn from them. Think carefully before responding to your child when he has struggled or not done his best at home or school. Mary Cay Ricci, author of *Mindsets in the Classroom* (2013), suggested adopting a "glass half full" mentality in the home and focusing on positives.

+ Praise your child's effort, hard work, and perseverance and not the end result, such as winning first place in the contest or scoring 100% on a test. Carol Dweck, author of *Mindset: The New Psychology of Success* (2006), discussed what constitutes an appropriate type of praise for children:

> Should we try to restrain our admiration for their successes? Not at all. It just means that we should keep away from a certain *kind* of praise—praise that judges their intelligence or talent. Or praise that implies that we're proud of them for their intelligence or talent rather than for the work they put in. We can praise them as much as we want for growth oriented process—what they accomplished through practice, study, persistence, and good strategies. And we can ask them about their work in a way that admires and appreciates their efforts and choices. (p. 177)

+ Encourage your child to participate in activities, hobbies, or even new subjects that require him to stretch out of a comfort zone and try something new. Find family activities that everyone enjoys as you learn together. Don't protect a perfectionist child from failure but rather teach her how to handle challenges and learn from her mistakes. Encourage your child to realize his own limitations and possible asynchronous areas of development; for instance, he may be very talented in math and music, but not be gifted in writing (or even struggle with writing).

Implications for School

+ Make sure your child with perfectionist tendencies completes projects on her own; as a parent, don't jump in to help quickly in order to avoid stress. As Jill Adelson and Hope Wilson (2009) stated, "When a parent jumps in and completes the project or assignment, it reinforces the child's ideas about the need for perfection, elimination of all errors, and his or her own inadequacy" (p. 147). Rather, find a quiet place to work, de-emphasize the emotions, and encourage task completion. Give your child a snack, play quiet music, or have him work at the kitchen table, so you can check in periodically but not hover or take over with the glue, scissors, or glitter to "help" your child.

+ De-emphasize grades and celebrate learning and growth, not perfection or A's. Encourage risk-taking and trying new things, whether that means a new club, sport, or musical instrument.

+ Communicate regularly with both your child and your child's teachers. Allow your child time and give him your undivided attention as he talks about stresses and challenges. Discuss how to handle the stressors in a positive way. Ask your child's teachers to give praise messages that value effort as much as achievement. Discuss the teacher's expectations for your child's achievement; if your child has mastered the class content, for instance, ask about extensions that might challenge her to learn new information or apply the learning in a new way. Communicate with the teachers about the level of stress, perfectionism, and challenges with your child. Open lines of communication between you, your child, and your child's teachers will help make for a positive learning experience.

"I found myself most content when my children reached the point where they had become comfortable with who they were and the skill set they had been given. It happened at different ages and under different circumstances for each child, but the transformation was undeniable and quite a relief for both the child and the parent."
—Karen Bickett, parent

Growth Versus Fixed Mindset

A critical component of responding to your gifted child's social and emotional needs and managing the implications of those needs both at home and in school is understanding the difference between a growth mindset and a fixed mindset, terms coined by psychologist Carol Dweck (2006). Mary Cay Ricci (2013) defined a fixed mindset as "a belief system that suggests that a person has a predetermined amount of intelligence, skills, or talents" (p. 3). This mindset, according to Dweck (2006), "leads to a desire to look smart and therefore a tendency to avoid challenges, get defensive or give up easily, see effort as fruitless or worse, ignore useful negative feedback, and feel threatened by the success of others" (p. 245).

A growth mindset, on the other hand, is "a belief system that suggests that one's intelligence can be grown or developed with persistence, effort, and a focus on learning" (Ricci, 2013, p. 3). A growth mindset encourages persistence through challenges, a desire to learn and embrace change, and a focus on effort to achieve goals. Understanding the difference in these two mindsets and embracing the growth mindset for yourself and in your role as a parent is vital to successfully promoting this mindset in your gifted child.

Final Thoughts

Parenting a gifted child, one who may experience the world in a much more intense way, one who is capable of empathy and emotional responses well beyond his chronological years, one who may have one or more OEs, or one who has a drive for perfectionism that affects her actions at school and home can be both a blessing and a challenge. Our role as parents not only influences that child's view of the world but also influences the skills he or she acquires to navigate it effectively.

Implications for Home

+ Emphasize hard work and build a growth mindset in yourself in order to cultivate that in your child. Praise your child with statements such as "you worked so hard" rather than "you are so smart." Ricci (2013) described the impact of the fixed/growth mindset on family dynamics:

> It is not surprising to note that parents also have a big impact on how children view themselves. They will often view their children through specific lenses: "Joseph was born knowing his math facts," "Domenic has always asked good questions," and "Catherine just knows how to interpret a piece of literature." These are all examples of a fixed mindset, even though the statements sound positive. These statements describe who these children "are," not the effort that they have put forth. (p. 4)

+ Make sure to communicate with your child, focusing on strengths, being nonjudgmental, and demonstrating active listening techniques. Ask open-ended questions to encourage your child to lead the conversation about his successes and challenges. Dweck (2006) encouraged this open, nonjudgmental communication, stressing that

> every word and action can send a message. It tells children—or students, or athletes—how to think about themselves. It can be a fixed-mindset message that says: *You have permanent traits and I'm judging them.* Or it can be a growth-mindset message that says: *You are a developing person and I am interested in your development.* (p. 172)

Implications for School

+ Make sure that the teacher is providing continuous learning opportunities for your child. If your child already knows how to read when starting kindergarten, for instance, learning letters is not challenging or appropriate. Different, more appropriate learning experiences should be provided so your child is continually progressing with new skills or content. Often, social and emotional problems occur for gifted kids in school because of their unique cognitive learning needs. Gifted researchers Nancy Robinson, Sally Reis, Maureen Neihart, and Sidney Moon (2002) described the relationship between these traits:

> When social and emotional problems related to an individual's giftedness do occur . . . . they most frequently reflect the interaction of an ill-fitting environment with an individual's personal characteristics . . . . Most of their school days are spent relearning material they have already mastered or could master in a fraction of the time that it takes their chronological peers. Therefore, many never learn strategies to cope with the challenges related to effort and perseverance that other children encounter throughout their childhood and later lives. In addition, the maturity of their personal outlook, which is, in many ways, similar to that of older students, may result in a mismatch, not only with the curriculum, but also with their classmates. (p. 268)

For More Information

+ *Mindset: The New Psychology of Success* by Carol Dweck (Ballantine Books, 2007)—Dweck's book discusses fixed and growth mindsets and implications of both.
+ *Mindsets in the Classroom: Building a Culture of Success and Student Achievement in School* by Mary Cay Ricci (Prufrock

Press, 2013)—This is a great resource on ways mindsets affect both teaching and learning. Ricci also has a book designed especially for educators: *Ready-to-Use Resources for Mindsets in the Classroom: Everything Educators Need for Classroom Success* (Prufrock Press, 2015). You may be most interested in her latest book for parents: *Mindsets for Parents: Strategies to Encourage Growth Mindsets in Kids* (Prufrock Press, 2016).

+ *Letting Go of Perfect: Overcoming Perfectionism in Kids* by Jill Adelson and Hope Wilson (Prufrock Press, 2009)— *Letting Go of Perfect* provides strategies for identifying perfectionism in kids and strategies for parents and teachers.

+ "Social & Emotional Issues" by NAGC—The NAGC site has more information on social and emotional needs of gifted kids at http://www.nagc.org/resources-publications/resources-parents/social-emotional-issues.

+ "Social and Emotional Characteristics of Gifted Students: Smooth Sailing, Rough Seas" by Duke TIP (2012)—This video, available at https://vimeo.com/41707896, provides an overview of social and emotional traits of gifted kids.

chapter 5

What Should School Look Like for My Child?

Our greatest success has been in providing professional development for teachers so that they understand the nature and needs of gifted students. We have also provided time for teachers to plan together and develop individualized gifted student service plans with goals based on data. We track the progress of our gifted students just like we track the progress of our students who are performing below grade level. We want all students to make continuous progress.

—Mary Evans, elementary school principal

Students with gifts and talents in Mary Evans's school tend to thrive because, as the instructional leader in the school, she understands the cognitive, social, and emotional needs of children and realizes the importance of her staff understanding this (and acting on that knowledge) as well. Not only does she provide professional development in gifted education for her staff, but she also includes interview questions about talent development to potential employees. Educational leaders well versed in best practices in gifted education encourage continuous growth in all teachers and in all students, including those with gifts and talents. What does that look like in a school?

A wonderful starting point for schools is the *Pre-K–Grade 12 Gifted Education Programming Standards* (NAGC, 2010). This work outlines six main standards: learning and development, assessment, curriculum and instruction, learning environments, programming, and professional development. Divided into specific student-based outcomes,

DOI: 10.4324/9781003237013-6

these standards also describe evidence-based practices recommended for educators to reach these outcomes. For example, under Curriculum and Instruction's section on curriculum planning, Student Outcome 3.1 reads "Students with gifts and talents demonstrate growth commensurate with aptitude during the school year" (p. 4). The evidence-based practices for educators include tasks such as "Educators design differentiated curricula that incorporate advanced, conceptually challenging, in-depth, distinctive, and complex content for students with gifts and talents" (p. 4) and "Educators use pre-assessments and pace instruction based on the learning rates of students with gifts and talents and accelerate and compact learning as appropriate" (p. 4). Read the Standards on NAGC's website. Although not a lengthy document, these standards prove foundational to best practice for your child's teachers. Imagine what could happen in a school that focuses on student growth based on aptitude alone—much less the other student outcomes!

According to the characteristics of gifted learners in Chapter 3, these students are abstract thinkers and problem solvers who thrive on complexity and challenge and who need little repetition of concepts. They learn at a much faster pace than their age-mates. Teacher Constance Baynum reflected, "They will become bored with school if there is too much reteaching. Give them opportunities to discover, discuss, build, and research." Because these exceptional students learn differently from their age-mates, schools must provide a variety of services to address their needs. Remember that the goal is continuous progress.

"I wish that regular classroom teachers could afford to spend quality time with their gifted students. It seems that the gifted students are often either used as peer tutors, left alone to work ahead, or doing all the work in collaborative group work projects. What they hunger for, though, is stimulating, engaging conversations about their studies. If they could get this interaction from their teachers, they'd be both motivated and encouraged."

—Jennifer Chaplin, district coordinator

Services

Problems arise when schools support gifted programs, not gifted services. Most districts coin acronyms, such as GATES (Gifted and Talented Education Services) for their gifted programs or give them titles like Project Challenge, and if those programs provide a wide variety of services, that is wonderful. Sometimes, however, the program is simply one service. For example, if a district only offers a pull-out program for elementary students where they meet with a gifted resource teacher monthly, those students are only served once a month (even though they are gifted 24 hours a day, 7 days a week.) Ideally other services should be provided in addition to this district's monthly pull-out, such as differentiated instruction and subject acceleration. (This chapter will discuss those options and more.)

Another pitfall of the term *gifted program* is that a person is either in a program or is not. District coordinator Jennifer Chaplin explained the importance of multiple services: "More than anything, I wish that all administrators would know that gifted children need intentional, daily services in their identified areas. While pull-out, enrichment, or resource services are important, too, gifted students need appropriate classes with like-minded and like-abled students and with teachers who have been trained in gifted differentiation." Varied services can address a multitude of needs as district coordinator Toddie Adams described:

My greatest success is having the freedom to meet the varied needs of my gifted students. Working with small groups at GT Academy or during GT/RtI (Gifted and Talented Response to Intervention) allows us to discuss social-emotional issues, stresses in school, academic issues, and personal triumphs on a regular basis. Students are challenged academically and creatively as each student's intellectual engagement is the goal of each lesson or activity.

Services for students with gifts and talents typically fall into two main categories: acceleration and enrichment. In short, acceleration involves a student moving more quickly through content, which may equate to finishing school before students of the same age. Enrichment involves the student going into greater depth or breadth. At times, these may overlap, so do not get overly concerned with which service falls into which category. The goal is to understand the variety of services that schools should offer to help your child make continuous progress.

Acceleration

As mentioned in the acceleration myth in Chapter 2, acceleration proves to be the most effective and cost efficient intervention for gifted children when administered correctly (Colangelo, Assouline, & Gross, 2004; Assouline, Colangelo, VanTassel-Baska, & Lupkowski-Shoplik, 2015). In fact, a longitudinal study (Wai, 2015) examined thousands of gifted students over decades and found that "exceptionally talented students benefit from accelerative learning opportunities, have few regrets about their acceleration, and demonstrate exceptional achievements" (p. 73). Most important to acceleration leading to student growth "is a consistent and sufficient educational dose across a long span of time . . . or learning at a pace and intensity that matches a student's individual needs" (p.73).

Acceleration services fall into two categories: content-based and grade-based. With content-based acceleration, students typically stay with their age-mates the majority of the day, yet they progress through the content or curriculum faster. They are accelerated in one or more subjects, such as a second grader moving up to third grade for language arts (called subject matter acceleration) or a seventh grader working at his own pace to finish pre-algebra in one semester and moving on to algebra the next semester (called continuous progress or self-paced instruction). Grade-based acceleration involves skipping an entire year, whether that is entering first grade early by skipping kindergarten, going from third to fifth grade, or gaining early entrance to middle school, high school, or college. These students typically graduate sooner than their age-mates.

Figure 5.1 outlines 20 types of acceleration with a brief description of each so that you can understand the terminology. It also contains a

Acceleration Option	Brief Description	Academic Effect Size
Early admission to kindergarten	Student enters school before the legal age as determined by state or district policy	+.30
Early admission to first grade	Student skips kindergarten or spends some time there but moves on to first grade his first year	+.30
Grade skipping	Student skips an entire year of school	+.67
Continuous progress	Student moves on to new content as soon as she has mastered the previous content	+.25
Self-paced instruction	A type of continuous progress with the student controlling the pacing	not available
Subject-matter acceleration	Student moves into a higher grade for one subject	+.42
Combined classes	Student works at the higher grade level within a split class	not available
Curriculum compacting	Based on a preassessment, student studies only those concepts not known in a unit of study	+.20

FIGURE 5.1. Acceleration options and effect sizes. Note. Types of acceleration come from Southern & Jones (2015) while effect sizes stem from the work of Rogers (2015).

Acceleration Option	Brief Description	Academic Effect Size
Telescoping curriculum	Through a deliberate plan, student accelerates through curriculum, mastering multiple years of material in one year or multiple semesters in one	not available
Mentoring	Student teams with mentor who provides advanced instruction	+.22
Extracurricular activities	Student earns credit in classes outside typical school day, such as summer programs	talent search programs +.34 summer university course +.43 Saturday classes on university campus +1.56
Distance learning courses	Student learns via computer class or correspondence class through an outside agency; typically there is a cost involved	+.72

FIGURE 5.1. Continued.

Acceleration Option	Brief Description	Academic Effect Size
Concurrent/dual enrollment	Student gets double credit for a class, such as middle and high school credit for algebra or high school and college credit for a college-level class taught in high school by a college-sanctioned teacher	+.41
Advanced Placement (AP)	College-level course taught in middle or high school by specially trained College Board teachers; advanced credit possible with passing grade on standardized test	+.60
International Baccalaureate (IB)	Student participates in IB program that offers college credit based on exam scores	+.70
Accelerated/honors high school or residential high school on college campus	Student attends high school designed for gifted students	accelerated/honors classes in high school +.69 residential high school +.29

FIGURE 5.1. Continued.

Acceleration Option	Brief Description	Academic Effect Size
Credit by examination	Student earns credit for a class through a performance measure or exam such as College Board CLEP tests	not available
Early entrance to middle school, high school, or college	Student enters school early	college +.23
Early graduation from high school or college	Student graduates in less than 4 years	not available
Acceleration in college	Student earns multiple degrees in 4 years	honors classes in college +.56

FIGURE 5.1. Continued.

statistic that may appear cumbersome to decipher, but it is very important because it shows how effective the acceleration option can be. The statistic shown in the chart, called the effect size, was determined by gifted education expert Karen Rogers's (2015) meta-analysis of research on acceleration (a meta-analysis is systemic review of all research done on a specific topic over a period of years). An effect size indicates how large of an impact the treatment (for example, grade acceleration or mentoring) had on learning. Look at it in terms of additional months of learning that occurred. For instance, an effect size of .4 indicates students gain 4 additional months of learning when receiving that service as opposed to similar students not receiving the service. See Rogers's chapter in *A Nation Empowered, Vol. 2* (2015) if you are interested in a detailed discussion of the studies included in addition to the effect sizes of the social and psychological impact of the types of acceleration (which are overwhelmingly positive). Overall she reported effect sizes for all subject-based acceleration for all grades:

+ academic effect = +.51
+ socialization effect = +.16
+ psychological effect = +.24

These equate to an additional 5 months of academic gain, almost 2 months of gain in social skills, and 2 months of positive psychological growth. Grade-based acceleration summary effect sizes were also positive:

+ academic effect = +.50
+ socialization effect = +.23
+ psychological effect = +.34.

The research is clear: Acceleration can be highly effective in terms of cognitive, social, and emotional growth.

Former district administrator and current director of a state residential STEM school Lynette Breedlove reflected on acceleration:

Acceleration is so important to children. Why must our kids always be grouped by age? What if the primary grades all did reading at the same time and split into reading groups by readiness? What if they did the same for math? The upper elementary grades could do the same thing. We are very assessment-driven these days but only seem to care about the end-of-year assessment. We use assessment as a gotcha at the end or as a worry stone about the gotcha at the end. If we really used assessment to determine what kids already know and allowed them to move on, we'd have lots of documentation to show they grew.

Former principal Kandy Smith relayed the importance of making acceleration decisions based on the individual child:

A family moved to our school system and came to enroll in the school where I was principal. The child had been in kindergarten in another state (labeled as gifted), but she was only four. Our state didn't provide for us to take her at that age or acknowledge the gifted certification at that age. My school psychologist wanted the family to wait until fall to send her. I disagreed, knowing she needed to be in school, especially since she had already been in kindergarten. I went to bat for her and her family, and we got her into school. She thrived.

Ideally, your child's school should have acceleration policies in place. These policies should include the use of the Iowa Acceleration Scale (3rd ed.; Assouline, Colangelo, Lupkowski-Shoplik, Lipscomb, & Forstadt, 2009), a decision-making tool that looks at the cognitive, social, and emotional development of the student in determining whole-grade acceleration. Not only should the policies be in place, but a variety of acceleration options should be available.

Enrichment

A second service category, enrichment, has been more loosely defined: "Strategies that supplement or go beyond standard grade-level work, but do not result in advanced placement or potential credit"

(Davis, Rimm, & Siegle, 2011, p. 126). Figure 5.2 outlines various types of enrichment and provides concrete examples. Enrichment basically manifests in three main ways in the school setting: as created or adapted curricular units, as curricular extensions, and as a technique for differentiating instruction (Gubbins, 2014). As parents, you should be aware of the types of enrichment used in your child's school. Some schools may adopt curricula (the actual lessons) and curriculum models (the theoretical foundation and components of the lessons) that have been specifically designed for gifted students. Curricula and curriculum models have been developed, implemented, and evaluated primarily through federal Javits funding for research in gifted education (as mentioned in Chapter 1). For example, "What Works in Gifted Education" (Callahan, Moon, Oh, Azano, & Hailey, 2015) examined a math and a reading study that incorporated several instructional models. The outcome was a blended curriculum model called CLEAR (Continual Formative Assessment, Clear Learning Goals, Data-Driven Learning Experiences, Authentic Products, and Rich Curriculum); curricula developed using this model proved effective with gifted students (Callahan, Moon, Oh, Azano, & Hailey, 2015). Ideally your child's school provides curricular units specifically for the gifted. If not, find out why (the answers can range from lack of knowledge to lack of funding) and see what you can do to help.

Another enrichment possibility is curricular extensions. Models have been developed that put theories of gifted education into practice, which can be an effective way for your child to have continuous progress. For example, the Schoolwide Enrichment Model (Renzulli & Reis, 2014), developed and researched over 30 years, emphasizes three E's that lead to higher achievement:

+ enjoyment,
+ engagement, and
+ greater enthusiasm for learning. (p. 2)

Schools provide general enrichment strategies to all of their students (called Type I: General Exploratory Experiences) while affording advanced opportunities (called Type II: Group Training Activities and Type III: Individual and Small Group Investigations of Real Problems) for those who are ready. Students are able to explore issues of personal interest in meaningful ways. Ideally, your child's school has adopted a formal enrichment model or, at the very least, has a plan in place for extensions of the curricula.

As parents, perhaps it is easier to find enrichment opportunities for your child outside of school than it is to provide acceleration possibilities at school. As Figure 5.2 indicates, many communities and universities offer summer and weekend camps and classes. Both residential and nonresidential, the opportunities cover all content areas from the arts and music to science and math. Not only do these give your child the opportunity to explore an interest, but they also do so in a nonthreatening environment—one without grades. Perhaps one of the greatest benefits stems from like people finding each other. For some, residential summer academic camps, for example, may be the first time a middle schooler finds another middle schooler interested in string theory or film noir. One parent commented about her son's experience at a 3-week academic summer camp:

> My son's self-confidence rose dramatically. Teachers trusted and enjoyed him; counselors nurtured him; peers made him roll laughing. Everything worked together! This program is, very quietly, life changing. These children stand out all the time. It's a blessing for them to blend in for a few weeks. Putting bright kids together in an environment where it's okay to be smart is a win-win situation.

Do not let cost prohibit your child from participating in such a win-win opportunity. Ask about financial aid; many of the sponsoring organizations or institutions offer help. State gifted associations sometimes provide financial aid as well. And don't forget local organizations such as the Rotary Club, Kiwanis, or churches. Many are willing to provide assistance in exchange for a presentation to the group or public acknowledgement.

Enrichment Option	Brief Description	Examples
Curriculum units	Intentionally designed learning experiences that remove the learning ceiling for academically talented students	Project M³: Mentoring Mathematical Minds (Kendall Hunt); *Exploring America in the 1950s: Beneath the Formica* (Center for Gifted Education, William & Mary, 2014); *Electricity City: Creating a City's Electrical System* (Center for Gifted Education, William & Mary, 2007)
Curricular extensions	Intentionally designed learning experiences that provide depth or breadth to content being studied	Schoolwide Enrichment Model; Purdue Three-Stage Model
Differentiation	Deliberate match of content, process, product, or assessment to student's readiness levels, interests, or needs	Tiered assignments; student choice based on appropriately challenging options
Competitions	Organized contests in all content areas	U.S. Academic Decathlon; FIRST Lego League; Intel Science Talent Search; Civil War Trust Essay Contest

FIGURE 5.2. Enrichment options. *Note.* Some options come from Roberts (2005).

Enrichment Option	Brief Description	Examples
Forensics	Competitive speech and debate taught in a class or club	National Debate Tournament; Individual event: Persuasive, Impromptu, and Duo
Problem-solving programs	Organized experiences and competitions emphasizing creative and critical thinking and problem solving	Future Problem Solving; Odyssey of the Mind; Destination Imagination
Seminars	Focused learning experiences on specific topic or concept; could be one-day or year-long class	Leadership seminar; creativity seminar; writing seminar
Pull-out programs	Students leave classroom to participate in learning experiences led by gifted resource teacher tied directly to their strengths and tied directly to content studied in class (also called send-out)	Five students gifted in social studies meet with gifted teacher during social studies class; they study the lives of soldiers and generals of the Civil War, creating journals and role plays while others study Civil War basics
Simulations	Orchestrated role-play experiences that mimic real-world situations	YMCA Youth in Government; YMCA Model Legislature and Court; Kentucky Youth Assembly; Mock Trial; class activity putting Brutus on trial for treason

FIGURE 5.2. Continued.

Enrichment Option	Brief Description	Examples
Independent studies	Individual learning experiences designed by the student in an area of interest; may last days, weeks, or longer	Student reads *Heart of Darkness* and completes high-level analysis during class study of imperialism; student conducts independent research on purchasing trends of teens in economics class
Extracurricular clubs and organizations	National, state, or local groups focused around common interests or goals; may or may not have admission requirements	Beta Club; Future Business Leaders of America; drama club; German club; LBGTQ club; Girls in Science
Community organizations	Local groups focused around common interests or goals; may or may not have admission requirements	4-H; Girl Scouts; Boy Scouts
Community opportunities	Academic, artistic, or social gatherings, events, or performances	Community youth theatre production of *The Crucible*; water color lessons at the community center

FIGURE 5.2. Continued.

Enrichment Option	Brief Description	Examples
Mentorships	The pairing of a student with someone more experienced or knowledgeable in an area of mutual interest	Online mentorship between a budding video game developer and someone who works at Nintendo; middle school student interested in politics meets monthly with the mayor
Weekend programs	University-, school-, or community-led academic or performing arts experiences; may last one day, one weekend, or several weekends in a row	Super Saturdays (four Saturdays of minds-on, hands-on learning sponsored by a university); district-sponsored one-day Winter Wonderland focusing on science
Summer programs	University-, school-, or community-led academic or performing arts residential or nonresidential camp; may last days to weeks	WKU's Center for Gifted Studies' The Summer Camp for Academically Talented Middle School Students; Center for Talent Development's Leapfrog; Duke TIP's Summer Study Experiences
Travel study programs	National or international university- or school-led trips that may or may not lead to school credit	Spring Break in Italy sponsored by a center for gifted studies at a university; an eighth-grade advanced social studies class travels to Washington, DC

FIGURE 5.2. Continued.

Differentiation

Can your gifted child's needs be addressed in the regular classroom? The answer is yes—but it takes deliberation, planning, and expertise on the part of the educator, and too few teachers have that expertise. In order to determine if your child is receiving differentiated instruction, you must first understand what it is. According to Roberts and Inman (2013), "A teacher who differentiates effectively matches the content (basic to complex), the level of the thinking process, the sophistication and choice of the product, and/or the assessment to the student or cluster of students" (p. 2). In order to do that, educators must ask (and answer) three basic questions:

1. Planning Question—What do I want students to know, understand, and be able to do?
2. Preassessing Question—Who already knows, understands, and/or can use the content or demonstrate the skills? Who needs additional support to know, understand, and/or demonstrate skills?
3. Differentiation Question—What can I do for him, her, or them so they can make continuous progress and extend their learning? (p 11).

To effectively answer Question 3, educators need a repertoire of research-based strategies founded on a strong belief that differentiation is important to student growth. However, even when they believe that it's important, they tend not to do it. A 1993 study (Archambault, Westberg, Brown, Hallmark, Emmons, & Zhang) found that teachers use one lesson plan to teach even though they voice the importance of differentiation; 10 years later a follow-up study had the same results (Westberg & Daoust, 2003). One factor affecting the lack of differentiation is that teachers simply aren't trained to do it. The New Teaching Center conducts the Teaching, Empowering, Leading, and Learning (TELL) survey across 20 states (New Teacher Center, 2015), questioning educators and administrators on a variety of subjects—including professional development needs. A large percentage of teachers have indicated that they need training on differentiation in order to teach their students more effectively, as these four randomly selected states indicate: Colorado 55% (TELL Colorado, 2015); Kentucky 57% (TELL Kentucky, 2015); Maryland 48% (TELL Maryland, 2015); and Tennessee 57% (TELL Tennessee, 2015). When teachers do have training, it tends to be focused on differentiating for exceptional students on the other end of the spectrum, not high-ability or gifted and talented students. It doesn't have to be that way. As elementary teacher David Baxter said, "The regular classroom teacher can provide gifted students with something new, something different, something engaging, something challenging."

Educators mainly differentiate according to readiness level (based on ability and prior study of concept or skill), interests (in the concept or topic to be studied or just interests in general), or learning profile (influences that affect learning: gender, culture, intelligence preference, and learning style; Tomlinson & Imbeau, 2010, pp. 17–18). For high-ability and gifted children, differentiation based on readiness level is the best approach for continuous progress and growth.

So what can you as a parent do if differentiation is the service option for your child? Ask questions. First ask to see the preassessment (that's the second question leading to effective differentiation, as mentioned previously). This should be an individual, written assessment before a lesson or unit begins that clearly shows what your child already knows about the topic, concept, or skill. It can take many forms, such as an opened-ended question or even the final test for the unit. How can a teacher differentiate if he hasn't ascertained previous knowledge or skills? If your child already knows 80% of the content, then he doesn't need to repeat it. He can't learn something he's already mastered. As principal Mary Evans said, "Preassess, then compact the curriculum and provide extended opportunities with lots of student choice—children should not have to spend time on material they already know."

After looking at the preassessment, ask to see the modifications. Is it just more work on the same level? If so, that is not differentiation. As fifth-grade classroom teacher Laureen Laumeyer explained, "Giving gifted students extra work beyond the normal classroom assignment is not differentiation; it is simply more work. Gifted kids are just like any other kid—they don't want to do extra work, especially if it is essentially meaningless busywork." Is the modification unrelated to the content the rest of the class is studying (such as reading a novel because she finished her math so quickly)? If so, that is not differentiation. Is it tutoring the other children who haven't completed the work? If so, that is not differentiation. The work should go deeper, be more complex, or have more breadth. District coordinator Dina Chaffin emphasized, "Strategies that you use in meeting the needs of gifted and talented students don't have to be big events. Some of the best strategies are small tweaks to curriculum that teachers can make every day." Sometimes those tweaks are so subtle that students do not recognize them for what they are: differentiation. That's why respectful communication among educator, parent, and child is key.

District coordinator Jennifer Chaplin emphasized the importance of students learning something new every day. She suggested that teachers "find ways to truly differentiate instruction. Replace curriculum; do not just add to the assignment. Modify methods. Find ways to accelerate. Allow students to investigate deeper. Do not use gifted students as peer tutors or teacher helpers." David Baxter advised educators to provide choice:

> Providing student choice is such a powerful vehicle for learning. I once had the opportunity to loop a group of students and incorporate project-based learning into our curriculum. This note from a former student, now currently in medical school, is one I will always treasure: "My education may not be over just yet, but I'll always remember fifth and sixth grade as the first time I took an interest in my own education and the choices I had to learn what interested me."

Elementary teacher Laureen Laumeyer agreed: "An open-ended project that enables the student to demonstrate his learning in the manner he chooses usually brings out the best in my gifted students."

Tracy Harkins, a parent of two gifted young people, commented on the difference differentiation made on her child:

When a teacher was truly caring and tried to adjust an assignment to meet my son's intellectual needs was when my child really soared. So many typical assignments at school are just mind numbing for gifted students. For example, my son really appreciated when a teacher would connect with him and ask if he'd like to do a more extensive research project instead.

Remember that differentiation can be an incredibly effective service. In some schools, it may be the only service. Differentiation is the vehicle effective teachers use to match content, process, or product to your child's needs, interests, and abilities or readiness level. The match is what makes continuous progress possible.

The Basics of Grouping

As a parent, it's important to understand the impact that appropriate grouping can have on student learning—and research supports this impact (Rogers, 2006). Before examining the types of grouping, please note that it doesn't matter how your child is grouped if the learning experience is the same for all groups. Whether it is through pace, complexity, depth, or breadth, the content, process, and/or product must be appropriately matched to the group of students in order to provide challenge and growth. That's the differentiation piece. For example, a teacher pretests fifth graders on multiplying fractions and discovers three main groups in her math class: a group who can readily multiply fractions, a group who understands adding fractions and is ready to learn multiplying them, and a group who is still have difficulty adding fractions. If she gives all three groups the same math problems, she is neither differentiating nor using grouping effectively. Each student group should get learning experiences commensurate with their readiness to learn fractions; each learning experience should provide an appropriate level of challenge.

Basically, students can be grouped according to ability or performance. Ability groups combine students who score similarly on some sort of aptitude or achievement assessment—like the previous example where students were grouped according to their ability to multiply fractions. Performance groups place students with similar grades or levels of performance together. For example, all students who earned A's and B's in sixth-grade math are put into pre-algebra. Both grouping methods have shown positive growth in high-ability students—as long as the learning experiences are a match. Sometimes these experiences are enrichment and sometimes acceleration, because many services can be provided in a variety of groups. Residential STEM school director Lynette Breedlove explained:

> Take off the learning ceiling. Find out what they already know, give them credit for it, and let them move on. Sometimes moving on is going ahead; sometimes moving on is taking a side road. Gifted children need the opportunity to do both. If everyone is doing the same thing at the same time, there are large numbers of students not getting appropriate instruction.

Look at Figure 5.3. The main types of ability- and performance-based grouping are explained. Karen Rogers (2006) completed a meta-analysis of research on grouping, and the research results in the figure stem from this. Please note the effect sizes; she considered +.30 or better to be significant (Rogers, 2014). Remember that a +.30 effect size equates with a three month additional gain in learning to similar students who were not grouped that way. In short, according to research, grouping students of similar high ability (that is ability-based grouping) or top performance (that is performance-based grouping)—and differentiating the curriculum for them—proves effective in student learning.

Final Thoughts

Schools should incorporate a wide variety of services to address the cognitive, social, and emotional needs of gifted learners. Ideally, both enrichment and acceleration options are provided as well as the intentional use of grouping. Hopefully, schools have policies and procedures in place to not only service learners who are gifted and talented but to

Grouping Option: Ability-Based	Brief Description	Research Summary	Academic Effect Size
Full-Time	Gifted students are placed in a full-time gifted class, gifted magnet school, a school-within-a school, or a special school	"clearly documents substantial academic gains and increases in motivation toward the subjects being studied . . . their perceptions of challenge and social outlets are substantially improved" (p.13)	Some studies show as much as 1 4/5 years of learning in a year's time. +.49 +.33

My greatest success was establishing a school for highly gifted students. It is amazing to see how powerful and positive school experiences can be for children when the environment really matches their needs. Students fluently verbalized how safe they felt where being themselves was normal—where they were fully accepted. Several students were identified as twice exceptional and were finally getting services for all their varied educational needs. Seeing the children's social-emotional growth match their academic growth was so rewarding. It was simply fulfilling to hear the students and their parents talk about what a difference the school made for them.—Lynette Breedlove, administrator

FIGURE 5.3. Grouping options. *Note.* Research summaries and effect sizes stem from Rogers (2006) and Rogers (2014). Multiple effect sizes reflect multiple studies. Direct quotes, unless otherwise noted, come from Rogers (2005).

Grouping Option: Ability-Based	Brief Description	Research Summary	Academic Effect Size
Cluster	5–8 students gifted in same area are grouped in the same class and receive differentiated learning experiences; rest of class is mixed ability	"substantial academic gains in achievement and . . . more positive attitudes toward learning" (p. 25); increased differentiation occurs; other students also benefit academically	+.62

Our greatest success came when we created a middle school academy designed for gifted learners. While it was a school-within-a-school, the gifted students were clustered for math, science, social studies, and English language arts. They also had one period a day to explore interests. They were given choices of topics for a 6-week study in which they explored the topic and created a product to exemplify learning.—Cecelia Boswell, district coordinator

FIGURE 5.3. Continued.

Grouping Option: Ability-Based	Brief Description	Research Summary	Academic Effect Size
Pull-out	Students gifted in same area are pulled from class by a trained teacher to work on extensions of content, critical thinking skills, or creativity	"substantial improvement in skill development....more differentiated materials are provided to teachers than for those in other grouping situations, thereby requiring so much less personal effort" (p. 16–17); students have higher self-concept	+.45 +.44 +.32

Personally, I am happy to provide them a relaxed environment where they are accepted and encouraged to discuss their ideas and theories with others. They crave new information, and they thrive when producing projects that share what they know with other students who are interested. They don't work for a grade; they work for knowledge when they're with me. And they work hard!—Constance Baynum, resource teacher

FIGURE 5.3. Continued.

Grouping Option: Ability-Based	Brief Description	Research Summary	Academic Effect Size
Cooperative	Gifted students are grouped together to work cooperatively on a task	"suggests possible achievement gains if and when the curriculum itself has been appropriately modified and differentiated. It does not seem to improve or harm self-perception or socialization . . . . there is no support that mixed ability cooperative learning groups has any type of benefit for gifted students" (p. 19)	+.28

FIGURE 5.3. Continued.

Grouping Option: Performance-Based	Brief Description	Research Summary	Academic Effect Size
Regrouping for Specific Instruction	Students in one grade are placed in classes based on achievement level in that subject; learning experiences are differentiated	High performing students can make as much as 1 4/5 year's gain in a year's time but curriculum must be accelerated	+.79
	It is being able to provide a homogeneous environment for those students identified as gifted in general intellect where interaction and learning can happen without fear of prejudice or being made fun of and where they are truly challenged. It's okay for them to be "smart" and "different" because there is a whole room full.—Penny Teague, resource teacher		
Cluster	5–8 top-performing students in an area are grouped in the same class and receive differentiated learning experiences; rest of class is mixed ability	Little research on this form of cluster grouping	+.44

FIGURE 5.3. Continued.

Grouping Option: Performance-Based	Brief Description		Research Summary	Academic Effect Size
	My greatest challenges with meeting the needs of my gifted students would be allowing them to work with other GT students to engage them at a higher level of learning. Since most systems divide the GT students equally among the elementary classrooms, they seldom have a chance to work together. While special education students are usually grouped together (due to scheduling), GT students are scattered throughout the remaining homeroom classrooms. While this makes a heterogeneous classroom, it does not allow the GT students to interact, share, learn, and challenge their thinking with others of the same ability.—Laureen Laumeyer, elementary teacher			
Within-Class/ Flexible	Teachers preassess and group students according to readiness to learn concept or skill; learning experiences are differentiated		Overall, research shows positive gains	+.34
	Gifted children are not a homogeneous group. They have different needs and skill sets that must be addressed within the classroom. Differentiation is still a priority even when these students are grouped together. One size doesn't fit all gifted learners.—LaTonya Frazier, district coordinator			

FIGURE 5.3. Continued.

Grouping Option: Performance-Based	Brief Description	Research Summary	Academic Effect Size
Cooperative	High-performing students are grouped together to work cooperatively on a task	Students complain less of lack of challenge, feelings of exploitation, and loneliness	+.28
Cross-Graded/ Multi-Age	*Cross-graded:* "All grade levels teach a specific subject at the same time of day so that all students can participate at the level in the curriculum where they are currently functioning, regardless of age or actual designated grade level" (p. 35) *Multi-age:* Students from three or more grade levels are placed in one class so they can work at own level	Positive for all learners; teachers more likely to accommodate differences; academic and leadership growth reported by teachers	+.45 +.46

Our elementary school is very good about ability grouping students during their core reading and core math instructional times. However, I wish they would consider full-time ability grouping. I also would like for ability grouping to not be the end of trying to meet the needs of gifted students. —Amy Berry, parent

FIGURE 5.3. Continued.

also identify these learners, especially from underrepresented populations. Optimally, too, all educators at the school have had robust professional development in gifted education.

Would-Should-Could Litmus Test for Learning Experiences

- Would most other students of this age want to learn this?
- Should most other students of this age learn this?
- Could most other students of this age learn this?

If the answer is yes, then the learning experience is appropriate for all learners; it is not differentiated for gifted learners. (Passow, 1982, p. 9; adaptation)

Implications for Home

+ Visit http://www.accelerationinstitute.org for a wealth of information regarding acceleration including the latest reports, the Iowa Acceleration Scale, personal stories, and more. The more you know, the better you can advocate for your child.
+ Seek enrichment opportunities out of school. Children need others who share their interests.

Implications for School

+ Read the 2010 *Pre-K–Grade 12 Gifted Programming Standards*. Share them with your child's school. Be familiar with them so that you recognize what services your child should be receiving. Go to http://www.nagc.org/sites/default/files/standards/K-12%20programming%20standards.pdf.
+ Make sure you understand the services offered in your child's school—and realize that sometimes there's a difference between what is offered in the policy and what is offered in reality. Ask questions. Be informed.
+ Don't be afraid to ask questions about differentiation.

For More Information

+ *The Best Competitions for Talented Kids: Win Scholarships, Big Prize Money, and Recognition* by Frances Karnes and Tracy Riley (Prufrock Press, 2013)—This resource provides detailed infor-mation about more than 150 competitions for gifted students.
+ Gifted and Talented Resources Directory—Visit http://giftedandtalentedresourcesdirectory.com for a listing of summer, weekend, and travel opportunities for gifted students. Duke TIP's Educational Opportunity Guide is also helpful: https://eog.tip.duke.edu. Also look at the Center for Talent Development's Educational Program Guide at http://programguide.ctd.northwestern.edu.
+ If you are interested in reading what the research says about best practices in gifted education, these two sources are wonderful:
    ○ *Best Practices in Gifted Education: An Evidence-Based Guide* by Ann Robinson, Bruce Shore, and Donna Enersen (Prufrock Press, 2006) is sectioned into three parts: home, classroom, and school. It is reader-friendly and robust.
    ○ *Critical Issues and Practices in Gifted Education: What the Research Says* by Jonathan Plucker and Carolyn Callahan (Prufrock Press, 2014) proves a bit more technical, but it is very rich and informative.

chapter 6

What Challenges Might School Hold for My Child?

I wish administrators knew that gifted children have a desire to learn something new every day—just like the rest of the student population. I wish they realized that gifted children should be allowed to work together (iron sharpens iron) to challenge their thinking. I wish administrators would stop assuming that the gifted kiddos "will 'get it' no matter what." I wish administrators would realize that these are our future doctors, engineers, lawyers, judges, and political leaders. I want my doctor to be smarter than me. I wish administrators knew that gifted children have just as many needs as special education students that are struggling.

—Laureen Laumeyer, elementary teacher

I wish that teachers knew that most of the gifted students already know what they plan to teach. I wish teachers knew that they are gifted all day, not just during a pull-out resource class or special gifted and talented event. I wish they understood it is their responsibility to meet the needs of these students in their classroom and would do what it takes for them to make progress.

—Dina Chaffin, district coordinator

Chapter 5 described what could and should be happening in schools for children with gifts and talents to thrive: a variety of services provided that are designed to match your child's strengths and needs provided

 DOI: 10.4324/9781003237013-7

by knowledgeable and well-trained teachers. Unfortunately, that is not always the case. Sometimes school provides challenges to your child—and not in the healthy sense. Note the issues Laureen and Dina mentioned: Belief in the myths discussed in Chapter 2, lack of challenge, lack of growth, lack of appropriate grouping, and more. Being aware of potential issues can help you address them before they arise.

Identification

The first issue to note is appropriate identification. Problems occur when a student is not identified when she should be, identified when she shouldn't be, or misidentified. Identification policies and procedures vary according to states and districts (see Chapter 1). Be sure to know policies, procedures, and your rights, especially in regard to due process and grievances if you wish to question any findings.

Ideally, multiple identification measures should be used with no one assessment standing alone. These measures should "align with both the definition of the target populations and the demands of the program into which students may be placed" (Borland, 2014). In short, demographics should be considered when testing choices are made (e.g., the Spanish version of an assessment can be used if needed, etc.). The type of services provided should also be considered when selecting students to be assessed. The goal should be inclusion, not exclusion. Not only should these measures include the more traditional achievement and ability assessments (both verbal and nonverbal), but also less traditional measures such as portfolios, performance-based assessments, observations, and checklists (by both parents and educators). Ideally, too, the measures used are valid: They actually measure what they are supposed to measure. For example, a school should not use an intelligence test to identify creativity nor should it use a verbal intelligence test in English to identify a non-English-speaking student. Optimally, blanket measures are given to everyone in the school, not just specific students teachers suggest so that everyone has a chance to be identified. Teachers tend not to be the best identifiers. District coordinator Jennifer Chaplin explained:

It seems that more often than not teachers are comfortable recommending students as gifted when the student is a "teacher pleaser." I would caution teachers to look for the students who know all the answers but do not intend to please the teacher with nicely completed schoolwork or well-behaved mannerisms. Look as well for the socially or emotionally immature or challenged students who test well but don't perform well in daily routines or work.

Best practice also dictates that students undergo blanket assessments multiple times in their school career (such as kindergarten, third grade, sixth grade, and ninth grade). Gifts can emerge as students mature. Ideally schools also screen all new students in their districts as they enter and not wait for the dates set in policy; imagine the gifted sixth grader new to the state who entered the school a few weeks after identification measures were given for the year!

If you are a parent of a child who qualifies for free and/or reduced lunch, speaks English as a second language, has another exceptionality, or is Hispanic, Black, or any other minority besides Chinese, Japanese, or Indian, then your child's chances of being identified as gifted greatly decrease. These populations are underrepresented in gifted education, so much so that the federally-funded Javits grants focus only on this population. For example, look at African American students, as explained by gifted education experts Donna Ford and Michelle Troutman Scott (2010):

> In 2006, Black students represented 17.13% of the public school population, but only 9.15% of those in gifted education—a 47% discrepancy. This percent is significant in and of itself, but takes on new meaning when translated into actual numbers. Specifically, these unidentified students equate to over 250,000 Black students who are not participating in gifted education. This is not a trivial number. Each one will be hard-pressed to become an achiever and to have his/her dreams fulfilled, because they are not placed in classes designed to meet their needs. (p. 2)

Don't be afraid to ask about the demographics of identified children in your school or district—the numbers should mirror the school's numbers. For example, if the school has 87% of its students qualifying for free and/or reduced lunch, then, ideally, 87% of the identified gifted students should also qualify for free and/or reduced lunch. *Equity* is a term voiced frequently in the field of gifted education as researchers, educators, and policy makers strive to improve both recruitment and retainment of underrepresented populations. In their chapter "Nonverbal Assessment and Identification," Kristofor Wiley and Marguerite Brunner (2014) said, "Acknowledging the varying cultures, experiences, and opportunities of students within a school or district can help educators make informed decisions about the 'right' combination of testing measures that will lead to valid identification practices for a well-defined program" (p. 476).

As a parent, be sure to understand the policies and procedures as well as your rights. You know your child better than anyone else, and you may very well be able to collect evidence for identification. Keep strong records: questions your child asks, anecdotes, evidence of work at home, evidence of activities outside of school, contests participated in, interests, etc. Gather letters of support from significant adults in your child's life like a private music teacher, the scout master, or director of the soup kitchen. You could also have your child assessed by a psychologist who understands gifted children. The results may vary from the group IQ test or other assessments given by the school. Note that this will be at your expense, and schools do not have to accept outside measures. Typically, though, schools are happy to have that information. Your goal is correct identification, which is the first step to appropriate services.

"I wish all teachers knew that gifted children need and build character from academic struggle just like the rest of us. If their curriculum is not significantly more challenging than the 'regular' curriculum, gifted children will develop poor work habits that will harm their development when they finally get to the level where the work is more rigorous."
—Keith Davis, superintendent

Services

A second major challenge for many gifted students is the lack of services or inappropriate services. As mentioned in the last chapter, know what the regulations and policies are regarding services in your school and district. Also understand what services are said to be offered as compared to what services are actually offered. Hopefully you will find a full range of acceleration and enrichment opportunities in addition to effective grouping practices, such as a self-contained gifted class, flexible grouping within a class, or a cluster-grouped class (see Figures 5.1, 5.2, and 5.3). Ideally you would have administrators who understand what district coordinator Jennifer Chaplin hoped for:

> More than anything, I wish that all administrators would know that gifted children need intentional, daily services in their identified areas. While pull-out, enrichment, or resource services are important, too, gifted students need appropriate classes with like-minded and like-abled students and with teachers who have been trained in gifted differentiation.

A powerful tool to use to match services to a child's strengths, needs, interests, and learning profile is an individual education plan, yet only nine states reported having such plans in NAGC and The Council of State Directors of Programs for the Gifted's *2014–2015 State of the States in Gifted Education* (2015) report. Parents often have input into the development and progress assessment of these plans, which can lead to more appropriate services. Find out if your state mandates them (go to the Gifted by State section of the NAGC website), and, if so, use them wisely. If not, you may want to advocate for the plans in your state or district.

Talk openly with your child about what happens during the school day. Then communicate respectfully with your child's teachers to see their interpretation of what happens during the school day. The two do not always mesh. Oftentimes services are provided that students do not realize because they are seamlessly integrated into the day, such as differentiation or grouping by readiness in a math unit. Remember that the vast majority of teachers love children and want them to succeed; work with the teachers if you have a suggestion for more appropriate services for your child. For example, if your eighth grader is not self-motivated, an independent study with little supervision may not be the best service. Or if your third grader has a passion for marsupials and a love of researching on the Internet, perhaps an independent study during science would be an appropriate match. The next chapter will help you to communicate effectively with your child's school as you partner for success.

Challenge

One of the greatest challenges facing the gifted child in the classroom is the lack of challenge. How many times have you heard your child say, "School is boring"? *Boring* may be defined in multiple ways: not challenging, too many repetitions of a concept (even a new one), too much time wasted when the work is quickly finished, no student choice, no student input, etc. Typically, though, students who complain of boredom lack challenge. Some students with extra time on their hands may quietly slip out a book to read or run errands for the teacher. Others find ways to occupy their time that aren't quite as socially acceptable; consequently, these negative behaviors often land the student in the principal's office, in detention, or even in suspension. Some children, like Tracy Harkins's teenager, are able to control their exasperation until after school: "Often my child would hold in all of her frustrations at school but then let it out at home. This took the form of screaming, defiance, and endless loop conversations." Other students lacking challenge may fake illnesses to miss school or simply skip class. Others become underachievers (examined in the next section). Unsurprisingly, behavioral issues often disappear for gifted students when their cognitive needs are met. Appropriate challenge is critical.

Figure 6.1 is a short article addressing the potential consequences of the lack of challenge. People may assume that lack of challenge in school only affects the amount, depth, or breadth of learning. It actually has a far more damaging impact than that. "What a Child Doesn't

What a Child Doesn't Learn . . .

Sometimes simple questions provoke profound answers. These questions solicit your immediate responses, and those responses multiply when several people are involved in the discussion, expanding on each other's thoughts. Some of these questions will also stick with you, and you will find yourself coming up with additional answers hours, even days, after the discussion. This one will:

> If during the first 5 or 6 years of school, a child earns good grades and high praise without having to make much effort, what are all the things he doesn't learn that most children learn by third grade?

This question has been discussed with groups of parents, in gatherings of educators, with students in summer programming, in meetings of superintendents and administrators, and in statewide symposia with key decision makers. The immediate answers are almost always the same. Those responses develop throughout the discussion, and participants leave a bit overwhelmed by the ramifications of the answers. It turns out that what a student doesn't learn can adversely affect him his entire life!

Take a moment to answer this question yourself, or have your child's educators and administrators answer it. What isn't learned? As you skim over your answers, you may be surprised at the sheer volume. But look closer and you may

FIGURE 6.1. What a child doesn't learn . . . . *Note:* From *Strategies for Differentiating Instruction: Best Practices for the Classroom* (3rd ed., pp. 205–209) by J. L. Roberts and T. F. Inman. New York, NY: Taylor & Francis. Copyright 2015 by Taylor & Francis. Reprinted with permission.

be astounded by the depth and weight of those answers—and the impact they make on a child's life.

What Isn't Learned?

Work ethic.

Books such as *That Used to Be Us: How America Fell Behind in the World It Invented and How We Can Come Back* (Friedman & Mandelbaum, 2012) remind us how readily Asian countries are bypassing us technologically, educationally, and economically. One main reason for this, according to Friedman and Mandelbaum, is their work ethic. They know that education and sacrifice are the paths for reaching a middle class lifestyle. They look at education as a privilege—and it is.

Everyone in America has the right to an education. Sometimes it seems, though, that our young people would argue that everyone has the right to a PlayStation®4 with unlimited playing time, a cell phone by fifth grade, and a car by 16. They may also argue they are entitled to an allowance and that days off from school are for relaxation and play and not chores. Experts argue that this will be the first generation whose standard of living will not surpass (or even match) their parents' socio-economic level. This is an entitled generation—or so they think.

How a person thinks about his talent and ability has an impact on his actions. Cognitive psychologist Carol Dweck (2006) argues that there are two types of mindset: fixed and growth. Unfortunately many mistakenly believe they are born with a fixed mindset, a certain level of talent and ability that cannot be altered. Rather, people should

FIGURE 6.1. Continued.

embrace the growth mindset, a belief that ability, talent, and intelligence are malleable—they can change through hard work and effort. "Without effort, a student's achievement suffers, if not sooner than later. Thus, it is important for students to value and believe in effort as a vehicle for academic success" (Dweck, 2012, p. 11). Our children must understand that without effort, success is fleeting.

Ben Franklin once said, "Genius without education is like silver in the mine." We could alter that a bit for the 21st-century American young person: "Genius without work ethic is like silver in the mine." No matter how bright, our children will not succeed personally or professionally without a strong work ethic. Working hard at intellectually stimulating tasks early in their lives helps to develop that ethic.

This first response is definitely lengthier than the others. That is because work ethic is the cornerstone to success.

Responsibility.

Responsibility is conscience driven. We make the choices we do because it is the right thing to do. Dishes must be washed in order to be ready for the next meal. The research paper must be done well and on time if we want that top grade. Punctuality helps us keep our jobs, so even though we choose to stay up until 3:00 am to finish a novel, when the alarm sounds a very short 2 hours later, we're up. Each day's responsibilities must be met to be a productive family member, employee, and citizen.

Early in life, we should learn the orchestrating role responsibility plays in our lives. And we also should realistically learn the outcomes when responsibilities are not met. It's all about cause and effect. If children do not live up to their responsibilities and if natural consequences are

---

FIGURE 6.1. Continued.

not enforced, we are not equipping children with this vital virtue.

Coping with failure.

To be perfectly frank, failure for a gifted child is neither an F nor a D. Sometimes it is a B—and sometimes even a mid-A! For gifted children (and for most of us), failure is not meeting the self-imposed expectations. Realistically, though, our greatest lessons in life often stem from falling flat on our faces. Through failure, we learn how to pick ourselves up and continue. We learn perseverance and resilience. We learn that we're not always right and that we don't need to be—that we may discover more through our failures than we ever imagined we could through our accomplishments! Dweck (2006) remarked: "Success is about being your best self, not about being better than others; failure is an opportunity, not a condemnation; effort is the key to success" (p. 44).

When we face obstacles early on, we discover how to separate our identities from the task itself—that means the failure of meeting the goal or accomplishing the task does not equal failure of us as people. Young people, especially those who are gifted and talented, must learn to take academic risks. They must learn to celebrate the outcome and be able to learn from the failure!

Self-worth stemming from the accomplishment of a challenging task.

We have all faced obstacles that seemed overwhelming, tasks that seemed too challenging. Giving up was never an option, so we worked and struggled and toiled until finally we overcame that obstacle or completed the

FIGURE 6.1. Continued.

task. The intrinsic rewards far outweighed the praise or even the pay earned at the end. We felt good about ourselves, our work ethic, our management skills, our persistence, and our ability. And even if the tangible outcome wasn't the promotion or "A" we wanted, that was secondary to the inner sense of accomplishment and pride we felt.

When students never work hard at challenging tasks, they can't experience those intrinsic rewards. Naturally, then, they focus on the extrinsic rewards. Unfortunately, being in an age of high stakes accountability only reinforces extrinsic motivation for students as they earn pizza parties for improved scores and best effort on statewide testing in the spring. Likewise, by giving them good grades for little effort that merits no intrinsic value, we're depriving them of this life-driving tool.

Time management skills.

Adults constantly juggle roles: parent, spouse, child, person, employee/employer, volunteer, neighbor, friend, etc. With each role come demands on our time and energy. Often these demands conflict with each other requiring us to budget our time carefully. Through experience, we have gained time-management skills by keeping track of the responsibilities of each role, estimating the time needed to meet that responsibility, and then following through. We adjust and readjust based on our experiences.

We know how difficult we make our lives when we procrastinate; likewise we know the sweetness of free time that comes from managing our time well. Young people who don't have to put effort into their work to earn high grades won't understand the time needed in order to develop a high-quality product necessary in more demanding classes,

FIGURE 6.1. Continued.

much less the time needed to do a job that would be acceptable in the work environment. Instead of gradually learning these lessons in schools, they may very well have crash (and burn) courses in the real world.

Goal setting.

We can't reach goals if we never set them nor can we reach goals if they are unrealistic. We also can't reach goals if we don't have a strategy in place that incrementally encourages us to meet that end goal. Students must have practice in goal setting and goal achievement. Those skills will impact their personal lives, their professional lives, their social lives, and even their spiritual lives.

Study skills.

Time management, goal setting, self-discipline—all of these are embedded in study skills. When children don't need to study (because they already know the information or they have the ability to absorb it as they listen in class), they never learn vital study skills. So when they are presented with challenging material, whether that be in their first honors class or, even worse, in college, they simply don't know how to study! How do you attack a lengthy reading assignment? How do you take notes in an organized fashion? How do you prepare for an exam that covers the entire semester's material? Yes, study skills can be learned, but like most things in life, the earlier we acquire those skills, the better.

Decision-making skills and problem-solving skills.

Weighing pros and cons. Predicting outcomes of possible choices. Systematically breaking down issues as to

FIGURE 6.1. Continued.

importance. Ranking possibilities and importance of crite-
ria. All of these skills come into play when making a decision. All of these skills come into play when problem solving.
If children don't ever have experience with this early on in
their learning, then when it is time to make decisions about
learning and life, when it is time to solve professional and
personal problems, they are ill-equipped to do so.

Sacrifice.

Yes, I would rather curl up with a wonderful read than
dig into my taxes. But if my taxes aren't completed by
April 15, I am in trouble. Period. I would rather catch the
latest Academy Award-winning film than bulldoze the dirty
clothes into the laundry room and lose myself for the rest of
the day. But wrinkled, dirty clothes don't go very well with a
professional image nor do they encourage lunch mates. As
responsible adults, we well understand sacrifice. Sometimes
we sacrifice our free time for our responsibilities. Sometimes
we sacrifice what we want to do because others wish to
do something else. We fully understand that we must "pay
our dues" in life.

But if young people procrastinate on assignments
because they really want to finish the Xbox One game or
text their friends and their shoddy work earns A's, they're
not learning about real life. Excellence requires sacrifice.
The IRS won't care that the reason your taxes were late
(and incorrect in just a couple of places) was because
you'd rather spend time reading a novel. Your potential
employer doesn't even want to hear the excuse of choosing to watch a movie over the preparation of your clothing
for the interview. Life's not always about fun or about what
you want and when you want it. It's about sacrifice and

FIGURE 6.1. Continued.

work ethic. It's about working your hardest at challenging tasks.

Final Thoughts

These answers to the question *What does a child not learn?* are only partial, and yours may well include values that this one didn't. What's particularly frightening with this one is that these are some of the most important concepts for a successful life.

So what does a child not learn when he earns good grades and high praise without having to make much effort? Simply put, he doesn't learn the values and skills needed in order to be a productive, caring person who contributes positively to our world.

References

Dweck, C. S. (2006). *Mindset: The new psychology of success.* New York, NY: Ballantine Books.

Dweck, C. S. (2012). Mindsets and malleable minds: Implications for giftedness and talent. In R. F. Subotnik, A. Robinson, C. M. Callahan, & E. J. Gubbins (Eds.), *Malleable minds: Translating insights from psychology and neuroscience to gifted education* (pp. 7-18). Storrs: University of Connecticut, The National Research Center on the Gifted and Talented.

Friedman, T. L., & Mandelbaum, M. (2012). *That used to be us: How America fell behind in the world it invented and how we can come back.* New Work, NY: Picador.

FIGURE 6.1. Continued.

Learn . . ." (Inman, 2015) poses a simple question: If during the first 5 or 6 years of school, a child earns good grades and high praise without having to make much effort, what are all the things he doesn't learn that most children learn by third grade? The answers tie to critical life skills so necessary for personal and professional success.

Take action if your child isn't challenged. Be concerned if your child brings home excellent grades, and you don't see effort going into homework. Suggest solutions; don't just point out problems. And by all means do not start the conversation with "My child is bored." You must partner with educators, not alienate them. Be prepared, however, that your issues may not be viewed as issues by your child's teacher, as parent Claire Hughes discovered: "My challenge was getting her teacher to challenge her—she has 100 averages, but if I complain, I get looks like I'm crazy." Remember that your child is probably sharing a classroom with struggling students, people reading well below grade average, learners with exceptionalities, and children with a host of other needs that scream for help. Because a gifted student's needs can be based on his strengths, not his deficiencies, he doesn't look needy (Roberts & Inman, 2015). Tips in Chapter 7 will help you communicate with your child's school.

"One parent told me her son's view of school was read a little, do a worksheet, blah blah blah, do another worksheet, blah blah blah. Another student said he was tired of talking about math, he wanted to DO math."

—Lynette Breedlove, administrator

National Impact

Not only should you be concerned about a lack of challenge for your own child, but you should also be concerned about a lack of challenge for America's children. Do you realize that very few students from underrepresented populations score advanced on national tests? Education policy analyst Jonathan Plucker coined the term *excellence gap* in the report *Mind the (Other) Gap: The Growing Excellence Gap in*

K–12 Education (Plucker, Burroughs, & Song, 2010) to describe the "large discrepancies in advanced achievement among children in poverty and from other at-risk subgroups and their more advantaged peers" (Betts & Islas, 2016). That report, plus the follow-up work *Talent on the Sidelines: Excellence Gaps and America's Persistent Talent Underclass* (Plucker, Hardesty, & Burroughs, 2013), emphasized that the highest performing students from lower socioeconomic backgrounds, who are ELLs, or represent a minority (i.e., Black and Hispanic) continue to lose ground, sometimes scoring two or three grade levels below their peers. In fact, if they continue at their present rates, those excellence gaps would take decades to close, if they ever would. Plucker (2011) suggested that policy makers and educators should ask two questions whenever they consider policy: "How will this impact advanced students?" and "How will this help more students perform at advanced levels?" (slide 38). He argued that "education systems that fail to develop the potential of students from every background can make claims to neither quality nor equality" (slide 2). We must develop and nurture all potential.

Underachievement

Underachievement means a "severe discrepancy between expected achievement (as measured by standardized achievement test scores or cognitive or intellectual ability assessments) and actual achievement (as measured by class grades and teacher evaluations)" (Reis & McCoach, 2000, p. 157). Some have speculated that up to 50% of the gifted population is underachieving (McCoach & Siegle, 2008). Why do children with such potential not work up to that potential? Sometimes it's simply because they lack opportunity. More typically, though, it's a choice:

> Students who underachieve may espouse one of three problematic beliefs: They do not believe they have the skills to do well and are afraid to try and fail; they do not see the work they are being asked to do as meaningful; or they believe the "deck is stacked against them" and that any effort they put forth will be thwarted. When students hold any one of these beliefs

they tend not to perform well. (Callahan & Hertberg-Davis, 2013, p. 383)

How do you know if your child is an underachiever? Not all underachievers possess the same characteristics, of course, but Figure 6.2 outlines several common attributes. Psychologist Sylvia Rimm (2008), however, argues that all underachievers are "consciously manipulative" (p. 6), whether that is manipulating getting out of work or pitting parent against teacher. (For an online quiz that helps you determine if your child is an underachiever, see For More Information.)

Can underachievement be reversed? The answer is yes; underachievement is a learned behavior and can be unlearned. Both counseling and instructional interventions are needed (McCoach & Siegle, 2014). Rimm (2008) developed the Trifocal Model from clinical experience and research in her Family Achievement Clinic. This six-step model consisting of assessment, communication, changing expectations, role model identification, correction of deficiencies, and modifications at home and school, typically takes from 6 months to a year to reverse underachievement depending on the dedication to the treatment (Rimm, 1997). Del Siegle and Betsy McCoach's Achievement-Orientation Model (Siegle, 2004), based on research in schools, examines four components necessary for student motivation and achievement: environmental perception (expects to succeed), task value, self efficacy, and self-regulation. "The blending of these two models provides excellent support for both research and treatment" (Davis, Rimm, & Siegle, 2011, p. 299).

If you suspect your child is beginning to underachieve, or if you've taken Rimm's online quiz and know that your child is an underachiever, take action immediately. Find out all you can about underachievement (see For More Information). Seek out counseling either through the school or through another professional who is knowledgeable about underachievement. Family dynamics often play a role, so be open to family counseling as well. Then partner with the school to devise a plan for achievement; instructional interventions are needed. In *Why Bright Kids Get Poor Grades* (2008), author and researcher Sylvia Rimm suggested the acronym ALLIANCE as a guideline for reversing student underachievement:

Characteristics of Underachievers

- Use reading, television, and video games as escapes from doing homework
- Have creative ideas which are rarely brought to closure
- Use defenses such as "school is boring"
- Disorganized
- Low academic self-perceptions
- Low self-motivation
- Low effort toward academic tasks
- Negative attitudes toward school and teachers
- Daydream and dawdle
- Lose assignments and don't turn in work
- Poor study skills
- Poor self-regulation
- May be perfectionistic and not finish their work
- May be interested in speed, zipping through work with little interest in quality

FIGURE 6.2. Characteristics of underachievers. *Note.* Information stems from Rimm, 2008 and McCoach & Siegle, 2014.

+ Ally with the student privately about interests and concerns.
+ Listen to what the student says.
+ Learn about what the student is thinking.
+ Initiate opportunities for recognition of the student's strengths.
+ Add experimental ideas for engaging curricular and extracurricular activities.
+ Nurture relationships with appropriate adult and peer role models.
+ Consequence reasonably but firmly if the student doesn't meet commitments.

+ Emphasize effort, independence, realistic expectations, and how strengths can be used to cope with problems, and extend possibilities patiently. (p. 153)

Practical and realistic, these guidelines can direct you as you assist your child in being an achiever.

Final Thoughts

You want your child to be an achiever. You want appropriate identification in areas of talent and giftedness. You want services that match your child's strengths, needs, and interests. You want appropriate levels of challenge for your son or daughter. You want your child to break an academic sweat. You want your child to have continuous progress and to become a lifelong learner. It's all possible; however, you must partner with your child's educators to make it a reality. The next chapter should help you partner effectively.

Implications for Home

+ Understand identification procedures. Know what tests are given and know what the results mean. Two great resources are Hoagies' Gifted Education Page's "Tests, Tests, Tests" (http://www.hoagiesgifted.org/tests.htm) and NAGC's "Tests & Assessments" page (http://www.nagc.org/resources-publications/gifted-education-practices/identification/tests-assessments).
+ Assist your child in discovering and cultivating interests. Take him to the symphony, a museum, an art gallery, a farmer's market, a golf match—the ideas are limitless! If cost is an issue, many museums have free times during the month while other experiences offer reduced costs. And be creative—your child can usher and see a performance free or be a page for your local legislator at no cost!

+ Provide challenge outside of school whether that be through music, sports, academic camps, etc. Enrichment is incredibly beneficial.
+ Do not rescue your child from challenge. Productive struggle is healthy and encourages the development of important life skills like persistence, a sense of responsibility, and problem solving.
+ Find out opportunities and share them: "Remember, opportunities are not real opportunities until you know about them" (Roberts, 2016, p. 2).

Implications for School

+ If your school or district does not have a gifted education committee, help form one. This committee can assist in everything from policy development to actual student selection to evaluation of services. Have the committee be responsible for quarterly reports to the administration and school board. Accountability makes things happen.
+ Be a powerhouse of information. Know regulations, policies, and procedures. Know best practice. Be a resource for the school and your child's teachers.
+ Share *What a Child Doesn't Learn...* (Inman, 2015) with your child's school, the school board, or any other entity that would benefit. It certainly debunks the myth that gifted children will be fine on their own.
+ Make sure others understand the excellence gap and its implications locally, nationally, and internationally. Ask policy makers and educators the two questions author Jonathan Plucker (2011) suggested:
    ○ How will this policy impact advanced students?
    ○ How will this help more students perform at advanced levels? (slide 38)

For More Information

+ Homeschooling gifted children grows in popularity each year. Many approaches exist. Be sure to be well informed of options for approach, curricula, and implementation. These websites provide excellent information:
  o Gifted Home Schoolers Forum (http://giftedhomeschool ers.org),
  o "Home Schooling Gifted Children" by Hoagies' Gifted Education Page (http://www.hoagiesgifted.org/home_school.htm),
  o "The Ultimate Guide to Homeschooling Gifted Children" by Raising Lifelong Learners (http://www.raisinglifelong learners.com/the-ultimate-guide-to-homeschooling-gifted-children), and
  o "Before You Decide to Homeschool Your Gifted Child" by Carol Bainbridge (http://giftedkids.about.com/od/educa tionoptions/bb/hsconsideration.htm).

+ *Why Bright Kids Get Poor Grades and What You Can Do About It: A Six-Step Program for Parents and Teachers* by Sylvia Rimm (Great Potential Press, 2008)—Rimm's book provides helpful information about underachievement. Her website, http://www. sylviarimm.com, is also an excellent resource. Not only does it have an online quiz to determine if a child is underachieving, but it also contains practical strategies and insightful tips on ways to reverse underachievement.

+ *The Underachieving Gifted Child: Recognizing, Understanding, and Reversing Underachievement* by Del Siegle (Prufrock Press, 2012)—Siegle's book is another excellent source for informa-tion and strategies to improve underachievement.

+ *Talent on the Sidelines: Excellence Gaps and America's Persistent Talent Underclass* by Jonathan Plucker, Jacob Hardesty, and Nathan Burroughs (2012) and *Mind the (Other) Gap! The Growing Excellence Gap in K–12 Education* by Jonathan Plucker, Nathan Burroughs, and Ruiting Song (2010)—Visit http://

cepa.uconn.edu/home/%20research/mindthegap to read both reports on America's excellence gap. You can also access your state's excellence gap report there.

+ Go to your state and district's websites to learn about regulations, policies, and procedures. Visit NAGC's "Gifted by State" (http://www.nagc.org/resources-publications/gifted-state) for legislative information, as well as state contacts in the departments of education and state advocacy organizations.

chapter 7

How Can I Communicate and Partner With My Child's Educators?

The major challenge I've faced as a parent of gifted children in school is knowing when and how to intervene to make sure that they are continually being challenged to grow and learn. I know I am my kids' first and best advocate, but there is certainly the fear of being "that" parent and how that may negatively impact my kids. When my second grader wrote a note to his teacher on his homework, "I need harder problems," I took that as an undeniable signal that I needed to set up a meeting.

—Amy Berry, parent

Characteristics of giftedness can create great successes and sometimes frustrating challenges for your child at school. Likewise, the myths of giftedness (see Chapter 2) can sometimes affect the experiences gifted children have in school. Joan Smutny, author of "Characteristics and Development" in *Parenting Gifted Children* (2011a), discussed the impact of these stereotypes in school:

The stereotype of giftedness—what it looks like and how it appears in the classroom—is still so strong that even the keenest observers tend to equate giftedness with achievement. But parents see much more in their children—the exceptional ability, yes, but also their heightened sensitivities, intuitive understanding, empathy far beyond their years .... Taken together, these characteristics can present special challenges in school. (p. 37)

DOI: 10.4324/9781003237013-8

Communicating with your child and your child's teachers is critical for helping her be successful in school (and, of course, successful means true learning, not just good grades). In order for effective communication and a partnership to occur, it's important for you as a parent to (1) be informed about what it means to be gifted, (2) have a clear message and purpose for meeting with your child's teachers, (3) create a plan together to best address your child's needs, and (4) be an advocate for your child and gifted education.

Be Informed

The first step in effective communication with your child's school is to be informed about the cognitive, social, and emotional characteristics of gifted children and the myths associated with giftedness (see Chapters 2–4). Resource teacher Ruth Kertis stated:

> I would like classroom teachers to be more familiar with the characteristics of gifted students. For example, gifted students are not always the highest performing students in the class. They are sometimes the students who are unorganized, do not complete class work, and are sometimes distracted or not paying attention to instruction. They also may be the students who have anxiety because they want everything they do to be perfect.

The better you understand giftedness, the better you can accurately share this information. From Chapter 1, you know that you must couple this understanding with knowledge of the laws, regulations, and policies in your state and school district. Research the National Association of Gifted Children (NAGC) website for information about the specific laws and resources for gifted in your state.

Equally important is knowing your own child. What are his unique needs and abilities? What personality traits and dispositions are critical to understanding how she relates with others? Be informed of challenges that your child's cognitive traits may pose in the classroom and on the playground. What happens if she has already read all the *Magic*

Tree House books, and the third-grade class is reading them in reading groups? What if he can already do basic addition when starting kindergarten, and class begins with learning numbers? Is your child mastering concepts quicker than peers? Does your child seem happy or frustrated with school? Knowing specific information about your child's traits will help you share them with teachers in a productive way.

It is also important to know your child as a learner and gather as much objective data as possible. Create a list of anecdotal data, for instance, such as examples of questions your child has asked, conversations he has had with peers, books she can read, or creative ways he has figured out a problem. Bring any examples of test scores, IQ data, achievements, reading or math assessment data, and school grades that you have available. Knowing your child's strengths and weaknesses as a learner will help you be prepared to have productive discussions with teachers.

Being informed as a parent means understanding characteristics of giftedness; knowing your child's cognitive, social and emotional strengths and/or needs; and being familiar with rights and responsibilities according to your state's laws and school district's policies. With this knowledge, you can develop a clear message as you meet with your child's teachers.

"My second grader's current math teacher is working to consistently challenge him and give him room to grow. I am so appreciative of the extra time and energy she is exerting to make school an actual learning experience for him. I just had a follow-up meeting with her to address challenging him more, and she's going to start him on the next grade-level standards. She's also advancing him with his social needs in mind, trying to find ways to challenge him within his class so as not to isolate him. For instance, he'll participate in whole-group instruction, but when it's time for individual work, he's completing more difficult problems or being challenged with critical thinking questions. She's developing a passion for finding ways to improve education for gifted kids, and my son is definitely benefiting."

—Amy Berry, parent

Have a Clear Message and Purpose for Meetings

In order to have a successful meeting with teachers and/or administrators at school, it is important to have a clear purpose and a specific message to share. For instance, if you are concerned about the social and emotional skills and needs of your child, ask for a meeting to discuss these needs and be prepared with questions to ask. If your message is that you feel your child is not being challenged, as in Amy Berry's introductory quote, be prepared to share that message with specific examples from your child's school experiences.

This may seem obvious, but it's important to emphasize: To communicate your message effectively, maintain a positive attitude and a respectful tone as you interact with teachers and administrators. Do not focus the meeting on things that are wrong but rather how you as a parent can work with the school to best help your child. Sometimes knowing how to maintain the positive focus is challenging, as parent Leslie Hutchinson stated:

> At my children's elementary school, I have faced the challenge of how to advocate effectively while maintaining a positive relationship with teachers and administrators. Since I have four children who either attend or will be attending this school, I feel I always have to balance saying what needs to be said versus maintaining peace.

One way to set a positive tone for the meeting is to begin by sharing successes or positive stories about teachers. According to Claire Hughes, parent and university gifted education professor, "When your child is lucky enough to get a good teacher, let the administration know how much you appreciate that teacher."

Mary Cay Ricci, author of *Mindsets in the Classroom* (2013), suggested the following tips to encourage and communicate a positive, growth mindset message (see Chapter 4) in meetings with teachers. First, always start with a positive statement, something your child enjoys about the school or the class. Second, share what strategies you use to bring out the best in your child at home. Third, share techniques you have used that did not work with your child at home and the reasons why. Finally, establish that you want to create a partnership to ensure the best possible school experience for your child (pp. 79–80).

David Baxter, teacher and father, described the importance of building positive relationships with teachers:

> I would encourage parents to advocate for their gifted children in constructive ways. Seek to develop positive relationships with administrators and teachers. It may be that your child's teacher has had limited training regarding the needs of gifted and talented students. Teachers are typically eager to do what's best for children, and you may be in a position to effect change, not only for your own child, but also for future generations of students.

To maintain a positive tone and a clear purpose for the meeting, it might be helpful to have some questions planned ahead of time. Jane Bush, district coordinator, stated:

> If you have questions about your gifted student's social, emotional, or academic performance, always approach the teacher in a positive manner so a plan can be developed, and the student can achieve to his potential. Many times the teacher, principal and GT resource teacher or coordinator can provide background on the student's performance and provide comparative facts that assist the parent in understanding the student's abilities and performance.

Depending on whether your focus is cognitive needs and academic progress or the social and emotional needs and development of your child, here are some questions that might be helpful to ask the teacher:

+ Cognitive needs:
    o If she has mastered the concepts and skills, how is she being challenged?

- ○ How are you providing continuous progress in learning for her?
- ○ How accepting are you of a barrage of questions if he is inquisitive?
- ○ If she has a passion for a certain topic, is there a time during the week when students share their interests?
- ○ Are there places in the curriculum where he might have a choice of the content studied or the type of product created?
- ○ What services are being provided to enrich the curriculum if she needs an extra challenge?

- + Social and emotional needs:
  - ○ Does she have a close friend?
  - ○ Does he play at recess?
  - ○ Is she participating in sports, music, or art classes?
  - ○ Is he demonstrating respect to teachers and administrators?
  - ○ How well does she collaborate with other students?
  - ○ Does she seem to be putting pressure on herself to be perfect?

Create a Plan Together to Best Meet Your Child's Needs

Being prepared for meetings with a clear message, purpose, and some questions related to the message will help you create a partnership with the school and teachers to develop a plan that meets your gifted child's needs. Mary Evans, elementary school principal, stressed the importance of building a partnership with the school:

We can work together to address your child's needs. Schools often don't have the resources and expertise to meet the needs of highly gifted students. We don't know your child as well as you do. Let us know what services you would like for your child. We may not be able to provide exactly what you ask for, but we may be able to offer opportunities beyond what is currently happening.

In Chapter 6, you read Sylvia Rimm's (2008) ALLIANCE guidelines for reversing student underachievement. She also devised an ALLIANCE for successful teacher-to-parent communication:

+ Ally with the teacher privately about your concerns.
+ Listen to what the teacher has observed about your child.
+ Learn about what the teacher thinks is best for your child.
+ Initiate a conversation about your child's strengths and problems.
+ Ask about experimental ideas for engaging and interesting curricular and extracurricular activities.
+ Negotiate to find appropriate adult and peer role models.
+ Consent to alternatives if experimental opportunities are not effective.
+ Extend possibilities patiently. (p. 189)

As you work to develop a plan to address your child's cognitive, social, and/or emotional needs, keep records and document decisions made in the meeting. At the end of the meetings, it might be helpful to reiterate or clarify what the school has committed to doing and what you will do as a parent. For example, what services will be provided for your child? How and when will those services be provided during the school day? How will they be monitored and by whom? How can you help your child at home? Planning follow-up meetings or discussions to track the progress of your child will help with accountability for all involved. Parent Karen Bickett stated, "I have found it refreshing to be able to openly and honestly discuss a child's strengths and weaknesses and work as a cohesive team in developing a plan that best fits the child."

"I wish that all teachers and staff knew the sad statistics about the lack of growth GT students tend to make in school (as opposed to their potential growth) and that they in turn would have the same sense of urgency to meet the needs of GT students as they do for struggling students. It seems that the attention always shifts to lack of growth for certain populations with the glaring exception of GT."
—Anita Davis, district administrator

Be an Advocate for Your Child and Gifted Education

Most importantly, you must be an advocate for your child! You understand your child's unique personality, gifted traits, interest areas, and learning needs better than anyone else. Parent Amy Berry discussed her lessons learned about advocacy:

One thing I have learned through trial and error is that I didn't advocate enough for my older two sons early on. Looking back, I can clearly see they both spent a significant amount of time basically spinning their wheels. I don't want that for my younger kids, so my advice would be to speak up sooner and more often for your child to be challenged.

Be involved in your child's school.
One of the best ways for you to be an advocate for your child is to be involved in your child's school as a parent volunteer, a member of the parent teacher organization or principal's advisory council, or any other type of leadership role available in your child's school. Tracy Harkins, parent, described her role in the school's governance structure:

Serving on the Site-Based Decision Making (SBDM) Council was probably the single most important thing I did to partner

with my child's school. Because financial and budgetary decisions are made at the school level in our state, having a voice
on SBDM allowed me to advocate for gifted students and
turn their needs into line items in the school budget. SBDM
Councils are also involved in teacher and principal hiring which
can greatly influence a school culture. I always encouraged
hiring staff that had experience in gifted or supported gifted
education.

Share information.

Besides volunteering or serving on committees, another way to
be involved with your child's school is to share information with the
school or teachers. Join professional organizations (such as your state's
gifted association) as a parent and share articles, blogs, and resources
with your child's teacher. Learn about opportunities at local universities
or museums and share those opportunities with your school. Provide
books for the school library or share information about professional
development opportunities for teachers in your area.

Locate and join an advocacy group.

It is also important for you to be an advocate for gifted education. In
Education of the Gifted and Talented (2011), authors Gary Davis, Sylvia
Rimm, and Del Siegle stated:

> Because gifted children by definition are a minority, in many
> cases adequate educational opportunities will be provided for
> them only if there is a vocal and visible support group in the
> community. If adequate G/T programs are not available, joining
> or organizing a parent support group should be a top priority
> for concerned parents of gifted children and for teachers inter-
> ested in gifted education. (p. 440)

Look for state or local gifted organizations or groups for parents of
gifted children in your area. Become familiar with your state's gifted laws
and resources in order to better support gifted education and funding.
LaTonya Frazier, district coordinator of a large urban school district,
recommended:

An option to find ideas and collaborate with other parents may be to join a local group of parents with gifted children. This will allow you an outlet and an opportunity to collaborate with parents that are raising gifted children. Check with your school or district gifted coordinator regarding opportunities to join a parent organization of gifted children.

Tracy Harkins reflected:

As a parent advocate I always felt it was important to advocate for all gifted children, not just my own. Sharing what I learned and banding together with other parents through groups such as my state's gifted organization allowed me to effect change in ways I could not have just as one voice. There is power in numbers, and I found the school district was much more willing to listen to our concerns if more families were involved.

This idea of power in numbers is humorously, but accurately, reflected in the following quote in *The Case for Parent Leadership* (Henderson, Jacob, Kernan-Schloss, & Raimondo, 2004):

+ 1 person = A fruitcake
+ 2 people = A fruitcake and a friend
+ 3 people = Troublemakers
+ 5 people = Let's have a meeting
+ 10 people = We'd better listen
+ 25 people = Our dear friends
+ 50 people = A powerful organization (p. 40)

By working together with others, your "powerful organization" can have an impact on not only individual teachers at your child's school, but also on gifted education at the school district, state, or national level. How is it possible to do that? The answer is by establishing positive, professional relationships with decision makers at all levels. Meet your school or district gifted coordinator. Communicate with your local school board members. Stay informed of state decisions and policies affecting funding and resources for gifted education. Know your state and national senators and representatives and ask them questions about their support of gifted education. Communicate with these officials, so they are informed about the concerns of their constituents.

Teach your child to be an advocate.

It is also important for you to teach your child to be his or her own advocate. In "Four Simple Steps to Self-Advocacy" (2011), Deborah Douglas explained how parents can guide their children through four steps of self-advocacy: (1) understanding their rights and responsibilities as a gifted student; (2) knowing themselves as learners using test data, interests, learning styles, and/or personality traits; (3) considering available options in their school, district, or community, such as enrichment classes, electives, Saturday programs; and (4) connecting with advocates or mentors, such as supportive teachers or guidance counselors. Douglas's suggestions, of course, might need to be adapted based on the age of your child. As a district coordinator and resource teacher, Jennifer Chaplin stated:

> I believe that the greatest service I can provide my students is the ability to be their gifted advocate and to teach them how to be their own advocates. It's also really important to keep a dialogue going their entire school career about issues for gifted students like perfectionism, underachievement, and academic resiliency. Understanding giftedness should be ongoing self-awareness for students.

Final Thoughts

We began the chapter thinking about ways to communicate with your child's teacher and school. What does it mean to do this well? It means being informed about gifted characteristics and gifted education; knowing your own child's cognitive, social, and emotional needs; using this knowledge to develop your message; partnering with the school to create a plan for your child; and being an advocate for your child and gifted education as a whole. In "Effective Advocates, Lifelong Advocacy: If Not You, Then Who?" (2011), Julia Roberts and Tracy Inman summarized this evolving process of becoming an effective advocate for your child and gifted education:

> An effective advocate doesn't just materialize out of nowhere. Rather, becoming an advocate is more of an evolution; you begin with concerns about your own child's learning. From there, you find kindred spirts who share those concerns. Together you craft a message that is communicated in a consistent, rational manner to decision makers. (p. 327)

For More Information

+ Visit NAGC's Gifted by State site to become familiar with your state's gifted regulations: http://www.nagc.org/resources-publications/gifted-state (see Chapter 1).
+ NAGC's Advocacy Toolkit site has suggestions for ways and resources to become an advocate for your child and gifted education. (http://www.nagc.org/get-involved/advocate-high-ability-learners/advocacy-toolkit).

chapter 8

What Can I Do at Home to Help My Child?

Follow your child's lead and feed his or her passions. All children are hungry to learn and inquisitive. Gifted children just seem to have a much larger appetite than others for knowledge and questions. Honor their quirks and intensities. They can't help it, but you can build an environment that helps them learn to cope and process through it.

—Lynette Breedlove, parent and administrator

As discussed in Chapter 7, you are your child's greatest advocate and encourager. Not only is it important for you to partner with your child's school, but there are also things you can do at home to support your gifted child's cognitive, social, and emotional needs. In this chapter, we will look at three important concepts for helping your child at home: (1) communication, (2) support and encouragement, and (3) age-appropriate responsibilities and choices.

Communication

Listen to your child.
The most important component of communicating with your child is listening. Because gifted children are often verbal at a young age and can have conversations about complex topics, it is important to make time to talk and to listen to your child every day. It is critical to understand how your child views and reacts to his world, whether

 DOI: 10.4

world is school in general, the bus, the playground, or science class. Debrief her experiences in school each day at dinner, talk about your day's highs and lows before bed each night, or ask questions during rides to and from school each day. Keep him talking by asking questions about what he enjoyed in the day, what his concerns or challenges were, or what good questions he asked. Toddie Adams, district coordinator, advised, "I always ask parents to stop talking so much and start listening and watching. Parents should listen much more than they speak. It is by watching and listening to children that you get to know them as individual people." Kelli Thompson, regional coordinator, offered this guidance to parents:

> Be perceptive. Listen to the verbal and non-verbal commu-
> nication your child sends about her needs and emotions.
> Understand how to address your GT student; she may not
> think in the same way you do. Learn how to best parent your
> child without frustrating him or her.

Encourage your child to take risks and to try new things.
You are your child's biggest encourager, and you set the environment to encourage a growth mindset (see Chapter 4) for your child and in your home. Often gifted children may be afraid to try new things because of the fear of failing or not doing them perfectly. As a parent, be open and encouraging for your child to take risks and learn new skills, even if they are hard and may be a struggle. Talk to him about making mistakes and learning from them. In *The Survival Guide for Parents of Gifted Kids* (2002), author Sally Walker discussed fear of failure:

> Some bright kids won't try anything new. They *hate* to be
> wrong, look foolish, or not know what's happening. They want
> to observe others in action before trying something new them-
> selves . . . . if your child's caution is prompted by a strong fear
> of failure, you'll want to help him feel better about himself.
> He needs to know that not being able to do something right
> the first time is *not* the same as failing and that even repeated
> failures or errors don't make him an inadequate person. (p. 53)

Allow your child to take new risks and try new things. Learn a new hobby together. Try a sport that the family can do together. Celebrate "failures" as learning experiences. Encourage the journey of learning a new thing and not the mastery of it. By doing these things, you are modeling for your child the challenge of learning something new, the normalcy of not having to be perfect at everything, and most importantly, the resilience to persevere through challenges.

Support and Encouragement

In addition to listening and encouraging your child at home, it is important to help support what your child is learning in school. As you work to develop a true partnership with your child's school and teachers, do your part to encourage and supplement that learning at home. The first step is to understand what that learning is.

Ask questions about what and how your child is learning at school.

See if your school has curriculum posted on its website or ask for a copy of your teacher's curriculum or unit overviews. Also pay attention to school or class newsletters or updates on topics studied in the coming weeks. If these aren't available and your child isn't one to share readily, ask your child's teacher for updates on what books they are reading as a class or individually, what math concepts they are working on, or what science or social studies lessons or projects are occurring during the year.

Also ask your child to share with you what her favorite subjects are. Make it a part of your daily family routine (maybe at dinner or in the car) to have everyone share something learned that day or something that piqued interest. Ask your child what questions he asked in class today or what she was curious about or thought about differently because of something in class. In their book *Make Just One Change: Teach Students to Ask Their Own Questions* (2014), educators Dan Rothstein and Luz Santana advocated the importance of having students ask good questions and develop their own sense of inquiry. Asking good questions allows students to (1) gain a better understanding of content and expand their learning, (2) develop confidence as learners and become more engaged in lessons, and (3) develop lifelong thinking skills to use inside and outside of school.

"The greatest joy of having gifted children has been the confusing feeling of understanding them, yet not understanding them all at the same time. Since I was identified as gifted as well, I completely understand feeling much more passionate about learning than one's classmates. I love that my daughter and I used to have spelling bees for fun and that we still delight in finding spelling mistakes on signs! I love watching my sons develop their own science experiments and having them beg me to buy Borax and food coloring for their weekend projects. I understand being different."

—Leslie Hutchinson, parent

Help with homework and projects in an appropriate way.

How do you successfully help your child complete nightly homework assignments or long-term projects for school? The first part of this process echoes advice earlier in the chapter: Know your child as a learner. Is your child the perfectionist who must always write neatly or paint in the lines in the perfect color? Is he the one that doesn't want to work the 15 math problems because he already knows how to do it after the first problem? Understanding your child as a learner can help you develop a positive homework environment to help manage potential stress.

In *Letting Go of Perfect: Overcoming Perfectionism in Kids* (2009), Jill Adelson and Hope Wilson discussed the following practical strategies for creating a positive homework routine at home. First, create a physical space and environment that is conducive to learning. Find a quiet place in your house such as a child's desk or the kitchen table that can be free from distractions. Make sure this space has the needed supplies or materials for the project. Next, develop a dedicated time for homework and be available to help or to answer questions during that time. It is important *not* to complete your child's work for him. Help develop a plan, help practice some problems with your child, help with suggestions, yes, but *don't* do the work for your child. Lastly, be sensitive to your child's daily routine and activities to allow for plenty of sleep, a consistent bedtime, and regular meals to make sure her physical needs are being met.

For long-term projects, gifted researcher and author Linda Silverman (2009) suggested helping your child (especially if he has perfectionist tendencies) to begin the project by establishing priorities, by simply getting started rather than procrastinating, and by developing a timeline for completion, including time management strategies to help achieve the priorities. She also suggested framing mistakes as learning experiences and modeling for your child how you tackle big projects at home or work by breaking them into smaller chunks. You should also advocate for celebrating effort and hard work on projects rather than the grade (Adelson & Wilson, 2009):

> Rather than celebrate on report card day, have a celebration at the end of the marking period before reports cards are sent home. This time should celebrate the hard work during the time period, rather than the child's achievement . . . . Celebrating the achievement of goals for each member of the family (parents included) sets an atmosphere that treasures hard work and completion of tasks. (pp. 151–152)

Finally, many gifted children may already know the content of the homework assignment or the project before they begin. In that case, think of ways you can help make the assignment more meaningful for your child. One family of a gifted fourth grader, for instance, decided to visit state historical sites during fall break so their child could use real photos and artifacts in her state history project that was due after the break. Also, remember that keeping an open line of communication with your child's teacher about assignments is important. You may need to ask the teacher if there are choices for content or products in the project or for different spelling words if your child finds the class list too easy and repetitive. Developing that partnership (see Chapter 7) with your child's teacher will help make these types of requests easier and hopefully more successful.

Provide opportunities to supplement what your child is learning at school.

Once you understand what and how your child is learning in school, think about how you can help supplement that learning at home. Regional coordinator Kelli Thompson suggested to parents, "Accept what schools offer your child as the minimum. Be an educational 'manager' of sorts for your child. Be aware of your child's educational needs and find the resources that can meet those needs." So what does it mean to be your child's educational manager? Three parents of gifted children described their view of the manager role in a variety of ways. Claire Hughes described it as "trying to show them a bigger world—and bring that world back to the classroom." Parent Leslie Hutchinson said it this way:

> Learn as much as you can. Be sensitive to your child's needs and listen. She will be telling you what she needs, either in words or actions. It may not be "typical" and may not be what your friend's child needs, but it is valid. My daughter needs to be reading six books at a time. She needs friends who want to talk about writing newspaper articles. One of my sons needs to spend time taking machines apart. At age 6 he needed his own tool box of real tools, so he could build the things he was drawing. We try to provide these things for our children just as we would provide food, clothing, and shelter, because to a gifted child, an unmet intellectual need can truly be harmful.

Karen Bickett described her experiences:

> I supplemented extensively with my first two children due to the lack of differentiation/gifted programming in their primary education. I tried to provide a variety of educational enhancement tools: books (both fiction and nonfiction), computer software, games, toys, puzzles, and exposure to educational experiences. I was also fortunate to have summer camps available to

my children, which allowed them to be with other high-ability children in a learning environment with educators that were both enthusiastic and knowledgeable about gifted education.

Notice that the common thread in each of these parent explanations is knowing what your child needs and being willing to supplement learning experiences in ways that are appropriate for your child. In her article "Differentiated Instruction for Young Gifted Children: How Parents Can Help" (2011b), author Joan Smutny explained that parents can supplement learning at home

> by creating projects that inspire creative thinking and reasoning, and providing resources that pique the child's curiosity and stimulate a hunger to learn more. Experiences like this in the home are vital for a young child's emerging sense of himself as a learner and instill, in his earliest years, all anticipation and excitement for discovery. (p. 226)

Provide extracurricular experiences based on your child's interests and passions.
Not only is it important for you to support your child's learning (cognitive needs), but it is also important for you to support your gifted child's interests and passions. Find out what your child is passionate about both at school and outside of the school environment. Does she enjoy talking to your neighbor who writes for the local newspaper? Does he beg to go to science camp each summer? Does she spend hours building elaborate Lego inventions? Does he spend time with a friend writing and acting out plays in the backyard? Whatever your child's interest, it is important to provide experiences and peers to encourage cognitive, social, and emotional growth and development. Jane Paulin, teacher, encouraged parents to "be comfortable with your child's interests, even if they're different from every other child you've ever known. Introduce your children to people who are passionate about what they do."

One way of introducing your child to someone who shares her passion is to allow her to choose afterschool, weekend, or summer activities and programs that match her interest areas. District coordinator

Dina Chaffin said, "Give your child the opportunity to 'find their people' through attending camps and events for G/T students." LaTonya Frazier, district coordinator, stated:

> Outside of school, gifted students need opportunities to participate in academic and social experiences that will allow them to pursue their interests and address their social needs. These children also need an opportunity to participate in activities that may not be of an academic nature (sports, music lessons, etc.) to develop the whole child.

Hundreds of opportunities for afterschool activities and programs are available through local schools, community organizations, and state programs. Whether it is sports, music, Scouts, Lego leagues, astronomy clubs, or school academic teams, look for opportunities where your child can meet like-minded peers and mentors. Find your local community's website for afterschool or community education programs. Watch for programs and speakers offered at local universities, libraries, or museums. Get on a listserv and/or mailing lists for national and/or state gifted organizations and check their websites periodically.

Kelli Thompson described the long-term impact of providing extracurricular experiences for her gifted daughter:

> As a mother my greatest success was to make my daughter aware of opportunities that were available and then provide the support for her to participate in the ones she chose. As a result of her K–12 experiences (e.g., State and International Academic team, piano, violin, cheerleading, tennis, 4-H, student council, homecoming court, summer camps, etc.), she was able to obtain a full ride academic scholarship. She is continuing to independently look for opportunities to learn and grow. That to me is success: when she chose her own path (not a carbon copy of someone) and then continued to refine it by learning all she can.

"Take them everywhere you go. Go everywhere that you can afford to take them. Many wonderful experiences are free. Be comfortable with your child's interests, even if they're different from every other child you've ever known. Introduce your children to people who are passionate about what they do."

—Jane Paulin, teacher

Age-Appropriate Responsibilities and Choices

Because gifted children often have the ability to learn faster than their peers and to have adult conversations beyond their age or years of experience, sometimes it's easy to forget that they are just children. It is important as a parent of a gifted child to remember her chronological age and the asynchronous development of skills and abilities as discussed in Chapter 3. Parenting gifted children effectively requires giving your child age-appropriate responsibilities and choices. Allow him choices or freedoms that are appropriate for his chronological or social development. Let her choose between two afterschool activities, for example, instead of presenting her with a list of 10 options. Psychologist Sylvia Rimm (2008) advocated empowering children gradually, using a visual representation of the letter V in the word *love*:

> Visualize the letter V as a model for guiding children. When children are small, they begin at the bottom of the V with limited freedom and narrow structure. As they mature and are able to handle more freedom responsibility, the limiting walls of the V spread out, giving them continually more freedom while still maintaining definite limits. During adolescence, as they move to the top of the V, they become capable of considerable independent decision making and judgment but should continue to recognize that there are adults guiding them. Thus they are ready for moving out of the V into young adulthood, independence, and personal decision making. (pp. 114–115)

In addition to providing appropriate choices and freedoms for your child, it is critical to implement guidelines and expectations for behavior. No matter how mature your child seems in certain situations and no matter how much she questions or argues with your decisions, setting clear and appropriate rules and consequences for behavior is essential for your child to develop the social skills necessary to thrive in a variety of settings. In a section of her book, humorously entitled "Coping with Young Lawyers," Sally Walker (2002) described this need for boundaries:

> Have you ever found a person three feet high who could out-argue your best efforts? If your gifted child is like most, he learned early to use his excellent verbal ability to get exactly what he wants. But just because he's good at it, don't let him dictate the rules and regulations of the house. Children feel more secure if their parents set a few important rules and stick to them, no matter what. Giftedness is no excuse for disobedience or obnoxious behavior. (p. 51)

District coordinator LaTonya Frazier expressed it this way:

> One piece of advice is to remember that gifted children are still children. Although, they may learn at a faster pace, they still have the desire to be accepted and affirmed. Provide them with opportunities to express themselves and give them choice with guidance.

Providing clear guidelines for behavior and "choice with guidance" may not always be easy with a gifted child, but it is critical in teaching her to adapt and to thrive in school and social settings.

Final Thoughts

The most important ways you can help your child at home are to listen, to accept and affirm his interests or passions, to supplement her learning at school with extra opportunities, and to allow him age-appropriate choices and opportunities. These tasks are not necessarily easy, but they are well worth the effort!

For More Information

+ Gifted and Talented Resource Directory—Visit http://giftedandtalentedresourcesdirectory.com for a listing of summer, weekend, and travel opportunities for gifted students.
+ *The Best Competitions for Talented Kids: Win Scholarships, Big Prize Money, and Recognition* by Frances Karnes and Tracy Riley (Prufrock Press, 2013)—This resource provides detailed information about more than 150 competitions for gifted students.
+ *The Best Summer Programs for Teens 2016–2017: America's Top Classes, Camps, and Courses for College-Bound Students* by Sandra Berger (Prufrock Press, 2015)—Published biennially, Berger's book is a great resource for summer programs for gifted students.
+ *Gifted and Talented in the Early Years: Practical Activities for Children Aged 3–5* by Margaret Sutherland (SAGE, 2012)—This resource contains numerous examples of activities to do with gifted preschool children.
+ *Parenting for High Potential*—This is a wonderful magazine that is published quarterly as a benefit of membership in NAGC, available at https://www.nagc.org/resources-publications/nagc-publications/parenting-high-potential.

chapter 9

What Does It Mean to Be Twice Exceptional?

Gifted children with disabilities continue to be ignored, programs for them are lacking, and their problems are compounded by sometimes severe social problems and rock-bottom feelings of self-worth and personal integrity .... It is indeed time to lift the mask. (Davis, Rimm, & Siegle, 2011, p. 398)

Chapter 1 established the fact that children with gifts and talents are exceptional children—those who learn differently from the norm. Just as a child can have multiple gifts, he can also have multiple exceptionalities, some that may fall on different ends of the learning spectrum. For example, does your child understand algebraic concepts at age 9 but have difficulty in comprehending a reading passage at the second-grade level? Does she create amazing contraptions at home, incorporating complex engineering design, but struggle with concentration and focus at school? This chapter explores the learner with multiple exceptionalities including gifted and talented, commonly known as twice exceptional, or 2e.

Defining 2e

The Individuals with Disabilities Education Act (IDEA; 2004), originally called the Education for All Handicapped Children's Act of 1975 (U.S. Department of Education, 2010), outlined different categories of disabilities:

 DOI: 10.4324/97810

A child with a disability means a child evaluated . . . as having mental retardation, a hearing impairment (including deafness), a speech or language impairment, a visual impairment (including blindness), a serious emotional disturbance, . . . an orthopedic impairment, autism, traumatic brain injury, another health impairment, a specific learning disability, deaf-blindness, or multiple disabilities, and who, by reason thereof, needs special education and related services. (Section 300 A. 1.)

A student identified as having one or more of these disabilities has many rights, including the right to have an Individual Education Plan (IEP) that outlines modifications to be made so that he can make continuous progress.

Students identified as having a disability also have the right to equal access to learning under Section 504 of the Rehabilitation Act of 1973. A 504 plan does not equate with an IEP, however. This plan is to "detail accommodations that need to be made to school buildings, classrooms, programs, or services to ensure that the student is provided equal access" (Besnoy, 2006, pp. 16–17).

Not all students who have disabilities require specialized instruction. For students with disabilities who do require specialized instruction, the Individuals with Disabilities Education Act (IDEA) controls the procedural requirements, and an IEP is developed. The IDEA process is more involved than that of Section 504 of the Rehabilitation Act and requires documentation of measurable growth. For students with disabilities who do not require specialized instruction but need the assurance that they will receive equal access to public education and services, a document is created to outline their specific accessibility requirements. Students with 504 Plans do not require specialized instruction, but, like the IEP, a 504 Plan should be updated annually to ensure that the student is receiving the most effective accommodations for his/her specific circumstances. (University of Washington, 2015, para. 3)

Many students with chronic health issues qualify for 504 plans and may not be identified through IDEA. The goal is that schools will provide equitable access to learning for all students, regardless of disability.

IDEA, when it was reauthorized in 2004, included the possibility of gifted and talented learners also having other exceptionalities (NAGC, 2009). The National Twice-Exceptional Community of Practice (2e CoP) defines 2e individuals this way:

> Twice-exceptional individuals evidence exceptional ability and disability, which results in a unique set of circumstances. Their exceptional ability may dominate, hiding their disability; their disability may dominate, hiding their exceptional ability; each may mask the other so that neither is recognized or addressed.
>
> 2e students, who may perform below, at, or above grade level, require the following:
> + Specialized methods of identification that consider the possible interaction of the exceptionalities,
> + Enriched/advanced educational opportunities that develop the child's interests, gifts, and talents while also meeting the child's learning needs,
> + Simultaneous supports that ensure the child's academic success and social-emotional well-being, such as accommodations, therapeutic interventions, and specialized instruction.
>
> Working successfully with this unique population requires specialized academic training and ongoing professional development. (Baldwin, Baum, Pereles, & Hughes, 2015, pp. 212–213)

A nationwide survey reported that only 14 states mention 2e in their special education and/or gifted education legislation, while 12 have it in policy (Roberts, Pereira, & Knotts, 2015). Acknowledging that children with multiple exceptionalities exist is the first step in identifying and serving them. Check the report to see how your state addresses 2e or contact the department of education.

"One million of our nation's most promising, most innovative thinkers—bright children who learn *differently*, not 'deficiently'—constitute a neglected national resource. Twice-exceptional children need an education that fits, and it's in all of our interests to give it to them."

—Micaela Bracamonte, parent and administrator

Identification

As mentioned in the 2e CoP definition, these children prove challenging to identify as exceptionalities mask each other. IDEA outlined 13 different categories of disabilities, yet the focus of research on 2e children predominantly examined those with Specific Learning Disabilities (SLD), Autism Spectrum Disorder (ASD), and Other Health Impairments that include Attention Deficit Hyperactivity Disorder (ADHD; NAGC, 2009). Roughly 50% of students with disabilities are identified with SLD (NAGC, 2009). Traditionally, these students have been identified using the discrepancy approach, which means there is a significant difference between a student's ability and achievement (which we know, from Chapter 6, can also be a sign of underachievement but for very different reasons.) School psychologists examine subtests of ability tests to see if scores have significant discrepancies or differences. For example, schools often use the Wechsler Intelligence Scale for Children®–Fifth Edition (WISC®–V, 2014) to determine IQ. A student may measure well above average in Verbal Comprehension and Fluid Reasoning Index on the assessment, yet score well below average in Working Memory Index and Processing Speed Index. Results such as these would be red flags for twice exceptionality.

Since the reauthorization of IDEA in 2004, schools use the Response to Intervention (RtI) approach to be proactive; instead of waiting for lack of achievement, intervention occurs before a student fails. If a student is not making appropriate progress, instruction or curriculum is adjusted. For example, if a student cannot comprehend what she reads on the second-grade level, her teacher may modify her reading to use first-grade reading level materials. With such a change, the student may start making progress in her reading comprehension. If classroom interventions prove ineffective, however, then students may be evaluated with achievement or ability testing and other measures. This approach tends to work well with average and below-average learners. For a gifted student, however, it proves lacking. From earlier chapters, we learned that a one-size-fits-all curriculum is not a fit for gifted learners. They need accelerated, enriched, or differentiated curricula. The RtI approach assumes that the curriculum appropriate for all learners is appropriate for the gifted. From earlier chapters we also learned that a gifted child making good grades does not necessarily equate with true learning—he may have already known the material. RtI assumes that failure indicates possible issues; this is not true with gifted students. The gifted child's strengths could easily allow him to make passing grades—even though the achievement does not match his ability (NAGC, 2009). In short, his work may appear appropriate when it is far from it.

2e individuals have a difficult time qualifying for Individual Education Programs (IEPs) and Section 504 Plans to receive needed intervention and accommodation. In a recent letter to State Disability Directors dated April 17, 2015, USDOE Special Education Director Melody Musgrove stated:

> we continue to receive letters from those with children with disabilities with high cognition . . . expressing concern that some local education agencies (LEA) are hesitant to conduct initial evaluations to determine eligibility for special education services and related services for children with high cognition . . . . Remind each LEA of its obligation to evaluate all children, regardless of cognitive skills, suspected of having one of 13 disabilities . . . (OSEP Memo 15-08; as cited in Amend & Peters, 2015, p. 245).

Schools must be diligent in identifying 2e learners. Parents, who know their children best, must be strong advocates, pointing out possible issues and documenting examples of discrepancies in what they are *capable* of doing versus what they *are* doing.

The following story relayed by parent Mary Alexander[1] exemplifies the importance of advocacy and persistence in getting appropriate identification and services. Mary described how her daughter Amy started talking late, but when she did start, it was in full sentences. This curious, highly mathematical child could neither spell her own name nor draw a circle by first grade. Testing showed that she would not qualify for services because she was not two grade levels behind—a state requirement for special education services. Finally the diligent school psychologist administered the Jordan Right-Left Reversal test, designed to identify reversal problem areas such as when children switch numbers or letter sequences. The school psychologist explained that she had "never seen a child try so hard or do so badly on the test," as she held up the torn test paper for the parents to see. Amy ended up spending the last 30 minutes of every school day with a special education teacher. After working with her, the teacher had her tested for speech communication disorders, and rightly so, for she scored a mere 1% in auditory processing. She excelled in this school where her strengths and her weaknesses were addressed until she moved at the end of her third-grade year. Her mom said, "By the time we moved, she still couldn't read, but she was doing math at a sixth-grade level."

From a military family, Amy moved schools frequently. Special education laws fluctuated so greatly from state to state that she sometimes didn't qualify. In her next school, in spite of the fact she was more than two grade levels behind in both reading and writing, Amy did not qualify for special education services because she did not score in the bottom 25% compared to both age and grade peers (a district policy). Neither was she recognized as gifted in spite of her math scores. However, her principal recognized the dilemma and orchestrated a plan, as Mary explained:

> The goal was to focus on reading and writing. Since she was so far ahead in math, the decision was made to have her miss math in order for her to attend two reading classes. Later the decision

---

1   Mary Alexander is a pseudonym to protect identity.

was made that she was so far ahead in science that she could miss that in order to work with the special education teacher on reading . . . and then social studies. Basically she spent all of her year working on how to read. It probably wasn't legal. It was the best thing that ever happened to her. Amy finally learned to read that year.

Fifth grade was a turning point for her. In spite of not reading on grade level, she no longer needed a reader. She won the regional Geography Bee and the school science fair. She scored in the 99th percentile on the Terra Nova in Science and Math.

In middle school, she won regional and state nonfiction writing awards, blue medals in Academic Olympics, and ribbons in the school science fair. By high school, Amy was in a state where she had an IEP—which prevented her from taking college prep classes in spite of her 146 IQ (another district policy). She actually had to prove herself in collaborative special education classes before she could take college prep and Advanced Placement (AP) classes—which she did. In fact, she was the only person in her school to pass the AP Chemistry exam with the highest score (5)—and she is still the only person in her school to have scored above a 3 on that exam. She graduated with 5's in AP Calculus AB, AP Calculus BC, and Biology—and a 1 in AP English Language and Composition; she scored a 35 on the ACT in Science and a 36 (perfect score) in Math—and a 21 in English. She was certainly consistent! Amy was accepted to every university she applied to and ended up attending one on full scholarship. She went on to receive numerous awards and is now in graduate school. Mary emphatically stated, "It is highly doubtful she could have done so well without the early intervention she received."

Note that this intervention simply didn't just happen—it took multiple people working as a team in a variety of ways over many years. Those professionals on the front line—typically the classroom teacher, but it may be a specialty area teacher—tend to be the first to notice discrepancies at school. Of course, parents may need to encourage them to look for those inconsistencies. The school psychologist, special education teacher, gifted resource educator, principal, classroom teacher, parent, student, and perhaps others depending on the individual student must partner together to identify and serve these 2e students.

Amy's challenges epitomize the 2e learner's challenges—difficulty in being identified as either having a disability or being gifted, challenge in having appropriate services that ensure continuous progress, and the importance of advocacy. Proper identification of giftedness for a 2e student can change not only her academic trajectory as it did for Amy, but it can also change self-perception. It can also change how she is viewed by other educational staff. District coordinator Jane Bush related this story:

> I worked with a student who could create and problem-solve the most detailed designs at an early age. My thoughts were this is an engineer in the making. His persistence and tenacity to stay with the project were exceptional. As early as first grade, he would lose track of what was going on in a traditional classroom. He would not want to participate with assignments because of extreme frustration. Teachers could not figure out what was going on with him and, at times, would say it was immaturity and lack of organization. His mother was determined to find his problem after 3 years of tutoring did not change his behaviors during the school day. After taking him to an outside agency for evaluation, he was diagnosed with severe Attention Deficit Disorder (ADD). Medication to make it through the day changed his world. He was formally identified gifted in General Intellectual Ability in fourth grade. Just knowing he had this identification changed his perception of self. Most importantly, it changed the perception of his teachers who now understood the ability was there, but he had a learning problem, so he needed a daily plan. He is thriving in the middle school setting at this time. He still goes to after-school homework assistance because he cannot always get his completed homework turned in on time, and the ADD still plays a role in his daily organization.

Parents and educators must not only be knowledgeable of twice exceptionality, but they must also be diligent in pursuing appropriate identification and services.

> "My daughter is twice exceptional—she is a gifted young lady with high-functioning autism. One of my greatest joys was having her giftedness be so significant that it helped her work around her autism. Incredible mimicking skills equal social success."
>
> —Claire Hughes, parent

Services

Once a child is identified as 2e, services should match the exceptionalities. Rarely can one educator alone provide all the necessary services:

> The provision of flexible, multidimensional, customized supports and services requires a system of education that is capable of dynamic and personalized interventions that respond to a 2e student's learning strengths and challenges. We believe that this kind of educational response entails more than an excellent individual teacher . . . it takes a team. (Coleman & Gallagher, 2015, p. 252)

Ideally this team builds upon the strengths of students, developing and nurturing their gifts and talents—not concentrating on the disabilities alone. Parent and university professor of special education Claire Hughes described her frustration with educators who focused more on her son's ADHD and Tourette syndrome than his intellectual giftedness. Her greatest challenges at school have been

> having his abilities recognized while not focusing exclusively on his problems; explaining that he's not lazy because one day he gets A's and then gets D's because he's disorganized or for-

getful; keeping him in the gifted classes even with poor grades; and having teachers not judge him because of his handwriting.

She advised parents to be advocates: "Keep showing them examples of your child's ideas—remind teachers of gifts and emphasize that you are trying to help develop those, not 'cure' his disability."

Services must address the whole child. So what might those services look like? Psychologists Jim Webb, Ed Amend, and Arlene DeVries suggested three fundamental approaches to teaching children with multiple exceptionalities: "First, . . . use remediation that will help to 'rewire' the brain, and teach skill development through instruction or . . . a tutor . . . . Second, use compensations—strategies that help a child use her strengths to work around areas of weakness . . . . Third, use accommodations where needed" (2007, p. 271). Notice the emphasis on using strengths in overcoming weaknesses. Micaela Bracamonte, who directs a school for 2e learners, outlined the crux of programming for 2e students in her article "2e Students: Who They Are and What They Need" (2010): "Nurture the student's strengths and interests; Foster their social/emotional development; Enhance their capacity to cope with mixed abilities; Identify learning gaps and provide explicit, remediative instruction; Support the development of compensatory strategies (Reis & McCoach, 2000; Smutny, 2001)" (p. 6). Services, then, should address the gifts as well as the areas of disability.

As a parent, what can you do about ensuring appropriate services for your 2e learner? You need to understand that, by law, you have a very powerful mechanism in place. This mechanism is the individual education plan provided under IDEA or the federally-mandated 504 plan. All public schools in the nation must provide services to students with special needs; however, special needs may or may not include gifts and talents depending on the state. A gifted services plan (when available in your state) may also be used to help ensure appropriate services are provided, but the federal mandates (and monies) for special education tend to be more enforceable than state and gifted regulations and policies. When developing an IEP, be sure to include multiple services to develop your child's gifts and talents. Also be sure to advocate for your child if the plan is not being followed or is not effective. Claire Hughes explained that she had to threaten to pursue federal action regarding her son when a teacher once claimed in an e-mail that "it was difficult to accommodate his 504" in a related arts area: "We had a meeting with the principal and threatened to go to Office of Civil Rights. Removing him from the class was necessary."

Another possibility for some 2e students is a school designed specifically for them. These places of learning, such as The Lang School in New York, founded by Micaela Bracamonte, tend to be private, independent institutions with financial assistance available in most cases. These schools look at all aspects of a learner. For example, Bridges Academy in California, a strength-based college-prep school for students in grades 4–12, employs a "holistic approach that acknowledges the dynamic interplay between and among . . . gifts, talents, and interests; learning differences; learning disabilities; social and emotional readiness; family context in which the student lives; and developmental asynchrony" (Baum & Novak, 2011, p. 8). Claire Hughes's 2e daughter ended up at a boarding school with such a philosophy, and she is thriving.

Final Thoughts

Parent, educator, district coordinator, and author Mary Cay Ricci described her son's twice-exceptional journey in Figure 9.1. Notice how so many of the elements—from difficulty in identifying to the importance of focusing on strengths—are embedded. Also note her persistent advocacy and her son's perseverance and ultimate success.

Implications for Home

+ Read Julia Roberts, Nielsen Pereira, and Dusteen Knotts's article "State Law and Policy Related to Twice-Exceptional Learners" (2015) for the results of their nationwide survey of states. Discover your state's laws and policies (or lack thereof) concerning 2e students. The more you know, the better you can advocate.

One Parent's Story

Around the time of third grade, my curious, persistent, happy little boy began losing interest in school. At the same time, his grades began slipping. After a parent-teacher conference, I could tell that Patrick was viewed as "average;" he was always on that wide "on-grade-level" achievement band and was not provided with challenging learning opportunities. He had been tested for GT at the end of Grade 2 and had a strong score on the Raven non-verbal assessment . . . but he did not hit the target score on the teacher checklist that was part of the screening process.

Patrick could talk his way out of a paper bag; he could argue critically and ask a steady stream of meaningful questions. I remember once when he was about 4 years old his Grandma was sitting on the beach with him. As a way of sparking his imagination, she pointed out a boat on the horizon and said, "Look at that. It might be a pirate ship." Patrick immediately asked: "How do you know? Can you see the pirates? Why is it at the beach?" Perhaps Grandma didn't respond in the gentlest of ways: "Patrick, you are so gullible." To which Patrick responded, "What is gullible?" Grandma had to explain until all of his questions were answered, and he was satisfied with his understanding of the word.

During third grade I decided that I would request an IEP meeting. I worked in the school system and knew that I had the right to make this request. I indicated that I believed there was a discrepancy between performance and ability. I will never forget that first meeting; that team looked at me as if I had two heads: Why did this mom request this meeting? Her son is on grade level. I shared

FIGURE 9.1. One parent's story.

that I believed that Patrick was both gifted and learning disabled, presenting work samples and anecdotal observations. Then I requested testing. I believe that the only reason they agreed to it was because I was an educator. He was given the WISC and Woodcock Johnson. His subtest scores on the WISC were all over the place ranging from 9 to 16 then later testing in seventh grade showed a range of 10 to 18. There was no question about recognizing him as both gifted/learning disabled with ADHD (inattentive type) as well.

What happened next was not surprising: an IEP was developed to address his disability and his ADHD, not his giftedness. School was not easy for Patrick. I had to understand that rolling across the floor while I quizzed him on vocabulary was what he had to do to memorize for a test. His grades did not reflect his potential; instruction did not engage him in the learning process. There were lots of tears and frustration. Even through all of this, I knew he would be fine if we could just get him through school. His mind was always going, and he had an entrepreneurial spirit. He negotiated Pokémon card trades in elementary and middle school, and in high school, he scoured thrift shops and online auctions for lighting equipment so he could be hired for various events and parties. When he grew tired of that, he began a car detailing business.

He went to a private high school and was accepted into a program for kids with learning differences. Many other GT/LD kids were in this program. There were a few teachers along the way that did recognize Patrick's spark, and they did provide him with more challenging learning opportunities. In most cases, Patrick rose to the occasion. For the most part, teachers just saw what Patrick could

---

FIGURE 9.1. Continued.

NOT do. One instance that stands out is when he was in a high school religion class, and students were asked to write a paper based on *The Sunflower*. This book, set in World War II, focused on choosing between compassion and perceived justice when a Jew is asked by a dying Nazi for forgiveness. Patrick wrote one heck of a paper. He has had an interest in WWII since he was in fifth grade. He had read many books and wrote a middle school research paper on the subject. He was so proud of the paper that he turned in! When the paper was returned, the teacher accused him of cheating—getting help or plagiarizing—because she had never see that kind of work come from him in the past and believed there was no way he wrote it. (There was a quick parent-teacher conference where I had to explain that Patrick has high interest in the topic, he did not cheat, and, by the way, the comments on the paper were inappropriate.) This teacher did not see any of Patrick's giftedness.

Patrick did not have a lot of choices for college because his grades were not impressive. He went on strike taking ADD meds because he said he was not himself when he took them. (I don't blame him.) He ended up attending a small liberal arts college. He started his college career as a media arts major but decided by sophomore year that he wanted to go into business administration. He knew it would be more challenging, and he was willing to take it on. Patrick graduated in 5 years in part due to the change in major and also in part due to having to take a few business classes over because a grade of D was not given credit in the business program.

Remember earlier when I said that I knew he would be fine if we could just get him through school? Well, 2

FIGURE 9.1. Continued.

weeks after graduation, after three rounds of interviews, he landed a job in his field. At the time of this writing, he has been in this job for 7 months and has been ranked number one in the country out of the 200 people in the same job. His disability is still there (still can't remember basic punctuation), but now he is in a place where he can demonstrate the giftedness that we always knew was there.

—Mary Cay Ricci

FIGURE 9.1. Continued.

+ Identification, as noted, proves troublesome. Read *Misdiagnosis and Dual Diagnoses of Gifted Children and Adults: ADHD, Bipolar, OCD, Asperger's, Depression, and Other Disorders* (Webb et al., 2005) to help you in that process.
+ Layne Kalbfleisch (2014) created a thought-provoking chart outlining skills typical of 2e learners and compared those traits in the gifted learner and the 2e learner. The "Twice-Exceptional Learners" chapter in *Critical Issues and Practices in Gifted Education: What the Research Says* (2nd ed.) is a helpful read.

Implications for School

+ Encourage your child's school to focus on strengths, not just weaknesses. After all, how many of us choose careers in our weakest areas?
+ For states that do not have individual education plans (IEP) for gifted students, be sure to address your child's gifts and strengths in the plan designed for the learning disability or other exceptionality. For those with IEPs, oftentimes the special education plan has more legal influence than the one for gifted.

For More Information

+ *Excellence and Diversity in Gifted Education (EDGE)* by Jennifer Jolly and Claire Hughes (Eds.)—The Association for the Gifted (TAG), a division of the Council for Exceptional Children (CEC), publishes this online journal, available at http://cectag.com/resources/excellence-and-diversity-in-gifted-education-edge. Published biannually, it includes relevant articles on educating the 2e child and is available at no charge.

+ *2e Newsletter* by Mark Bade and Linda Neumann (Eds.)—This newsletter, available at http://www.2enewsletter.com, is a subscription resource filled with invaluable information.

+ "Twice-Exceptional Learners," a special issue of *Gifted Child Today* by Julia Link Roberts and Mary Ruth Coleman (Eds.; 2015; 38 [4])—Articles by psychologists, educators, administrators, gifted and talented coordinators, parents, and students provide a rich understanding of the importance of partnerships in developing an environment where 2e children flourish.

+ "White Paper: Twice Exceptionality" by NAGC—NAGC created this white paper on twice exceptionality available at http://www.nagc.org/sites/default/files/Position%20Statement/twice%20exceptional.pdf.

+ "Tips for Parents: Twice Exceptional Students - Who Are They and What Do They Need?" by Dr. Edward R. Amend (2015)—The Davidson Institute for Talent Development posted this very useful piece, available at http://www.davidsongifted.org/db/Articles_id_10845.aspx.

+ *The Twice-Exceptional Dilemma* by National Education Association (2006)—NEA published this guide exploring twice exceptionality inside and outside the classroom. Access the report at http://www.nea.org/assets/docs/twiceexceptional.pdf.

+ "For the Love of Learning #18- Educating Twice Exceptional Children" by Raising Miro (Video; 2015)—Lainie Liberti, who runs the website Raising Miro (http://www.raisingmiro.com), also produces For the Love of Learning: Voices of the Alternative Education Movement, a series of educa-

tion videos featuring parents and experts, available at http://
fortheloveoflearningshow.com. You can find the episode on
twice-exceptional students at https://www.youtube.com/
watch?v=ZGWP0kpQbKw.

+ *Successful Strategies for Twice-Exceptional Students* by Kevin
Besnoy (Prufrock Press, 2005)—Besnoy wrote this book as
part of The Practical Strategies Series in Gifted Education, a
collection of short books written by experts in the of gifted field.

chapter 10

Where Can I Find More Information?

I think everyone would benefit from understanding more about gifted children's special needs. So many people think of high achievers and autonomous learners when they think of gifted children. They don't really understand the intensity and sensitivities that come along with high intellectual ability.

—Lynette Breedlove, administrator and parent

If you've read each chapter in this book, then you should have a strong foundation regarding your child or that young person who is important to you. From debunking myths to learning effective strategies to partner with your child's school, hopefully you are better equipped to advocate for your gifted learner. Although each chapter contained a list of resources under For More Information, this chapter highlights important sources (print and electronic); some have already been mentioned but are explained in more depth, while others are new.

Major Reports About Gifted Education

A Nation Deceived: How Schools Hold Back America's Brightest Students by **Nicholas Colangelo, Susan G. Assouline, and Miraca U. M. Gross (The University of Iowa, The Connie Belin & Jacqueline N. Blank International Center for Gifted Education and Talent Development, 2004)**—This seminal national study on acceleration for gifted students analyzed 50 years of research. The report discussed

DOI: 10.4324/978100?

several types of acceleration, addressed frequently heard concerns (or myths) associated with each type, and provided research from gifted experts and authentic classroom practice to dispel the myths. In short, it emphasized the effectiveness of acceleration for gifted students when implemented appropriately. Access the report at http://www.accelera tioninstitute.org/nation_deceived.

A Nation Empowered: Evidence Trumps the Excuses Holding Back America's Brightest Students by Susan G. Assouline, Nicholas Colangelo, Joyce VanTassel-Baska, and Ann Lupkowski-Shoplik (The University of Iowa, The Connie Belin & Jacqueline N. Blank International Center for Gifted Education and Talent Development, 2015)—Written more than a decade after *A Nation Deceived* (2004), *A Nation Empowered* (2015) explored 20 forms of acceleration, highlighted the research about the positive impact on gifted students' academic and social-emotional development, and included personal vignettes from parents, teachers, and students. Access the report at http://www.accel erationinstitute.org/Nation_Empowered.

Equal Talents, Unequal Opportunities: A Report Card on State Support for Academically Talented Low-Income Students by Jonathan Plucker, Jennifer Giancola, Grace Healey, Daniel Arndt, and Chen Wang (Jack Kent Cooke Foundation, 2015)—This report contained a state-by-state analysis of the learning opportunities and policies targeting advanced learners, specifically from low-income families. States were rated on the policies they have in place (inputs) and the performance of students (outputs). Unsurprisingly, scores were low. Access the report at http://www.excellencegap.org/research-reports.

Mind the (Other) Gap! The Growing Excellence Gap in K–12 Education by Jonathan Plucker, Nathan Burroughs, and Ruiting Song (University of Connecticut, Neag School of Education, Center for Education Policy Analysis, 2010)—Using data from national assessments, researchers showed statistics that defined and explained the excellence gap, an alarming achievement gap related to gender, poverty, ethnicity, and language background among students who perform at advanced levels. Access the report at http://cepa.uconn.edu/home/research/mindthegap.

Talent on the Sidelines: Excellence Gaps and America's Persistent Talent Underclass **by Jonathan Plucker, Jacob Hardesty, and Nathan Burroughs (University of Connecticut, Neag School of Education, Center for Education Policy Analysis, 2013)**—Written 3 years after *Mind the (Other) Gap* (2010), this 2013 report discussed the continued underrepresentation of low-income and minority students among those performing at the highest levels of academic achievement in the U.S. Using national assessments, researchers demonstrated that a large excellence gap still exists and continues to grow. Access the report at http://cepa.uconn.edu/home/research/mindthegap.

Unlocking Emerging Talent: Supporting High Achievement of Low-Income, High-Ability Students **by Paula Olszewski-Kubilius and Jane Clarenbach (NAGC, 2012)**—This 2012 report provided an overview of findings about the achievement of high-ability, low-income students. With sections on barriers, successful programs and practices, psychosocial skills for success, policies, and more, this report included a call for action from educators and policymakers. Access the report at http://www.jkcf.org/assets/1/7/Unlocking_Emergent_Talent.pdf.

Do High Flyers Maintain Their Altitude? Performance Trends of Top Students **by Yun Xiang, Michael Dahlin, John Cronin, Robert Theaker, and Sarah Durant (Thomas B. Fordham Institute, 2011)**—This longitudinal study followed two cohorts of students who were high achievers (high flyers) through several years of school and compared their progress and growth against their peers. It also examined which high flyers were most likely to remain at that status throughout school and how high flyers in high-poverty schools fared. Access the report at http://files.eric.ed.gov/fulltext/ED524344.pdf.

Diversity and Developing Gifts and Talents: A National Call to Action **by The Association for The Gifted, Council for Exceptional Children (2009)**—This 2009 report was a call to action for change tha addressed the significant lack of proportional representation of ethnic minorities and children of poverty in the numbers of students serviced as gifted and talented in the U.S. Authors discussed implications and goals for educator preparation programs, school services, identification processes, and areas for further research. Access the report at http://cectag.com/wp-content/uploads/2012/04/Diversity-and-Developing-Gifts-and-Talents1.pdf.

High-Achieving Students in the Era of NCLB **by Tom Loveless, Steve Farkas, and Ann Duffett (Thomas B. Fordham Institute, 2008)**—This publication shared the results of two studies about the progress of high-achieving students during the era of No Child Left Behind (NCLB). The report included an analysis of National Assessment of Educational Progress (NAEP) data, findings from a national teacher survey, and implications of the findings on high achievers. It argued that the achievement gap is shrinking: Lower achieving students move up while higher achieving students remain virtually stagnant. Access the report at http://edexcellence.net/publications/high-achieving-students-in.html.

achievementtrap: How America is Failing Millions of High-Achieving Students from Lower-Income Families **by Joshua S. Wyner, John M. Bridgeland, and John J. Diiulio, Jr. (Jack Kent Cooke Foundation and Civic Enterprises, 2008)**—With chapter titles like "Disparity at the Starting Line," "Disquieting Outcomes in Elementary and High School," and "Alarming Gaps in College and Graduate School Completion," this 2007 study shared findings about the educational disparities of U.S. high-achieving, low-income students from elementary school to graduate school using three national longitudinal studies as data sources. It argued that lower-income students score lower and lose more educational ground than their wealthier classmates. Only 28% of students in the top quartile of first grade are lower income, just 56% of that 28% will remain high achievers by fifth grade, and those few virtually disappear in high school. Access the report at http://www.civicenterprises.net/medialibrary/docs/achievement_trap.pdf.

Overlooked Gems: A National Perspective on Low-Income Promising Learners by Joyce VanTassel-Baska and Tamra Stambaugh (NAGC, 2007)—As a collection of presentations and papers by gifted researchers and educators attending the 2006 National Leadership Conference on Low-Income Promising Learners, this source contained a variety of perspectives on needs, services, and equity issues related to the critical issue of poverty and its effect on high ability learners. Priorities for action were included. Access the report at http://www.nagc.org/sites/default/files/key%20reports/Overlooked%20Gems%20%28final%29.pdf.

Visit the NAGC web page "Key Reports in Gifted Education" for an overview and links to several other major reports: http://www.nagc.org/resources-publications/resources/key-reports-gifted-education.

Other Valuable Resources

Online

National Association for Gifted Children (NAGC; https://www.nagc.org)—NAGC is the leading advocacy organization for gifted education in the United States. Mentioned several times in the book, this website contains information about many topics related to giftedness: characteristic of gifted kids, national and state regulations, identification, services, parent and teacher resources, advocacy tips, and more. While this website is free, becoming a member of NAGC has added benefits such as access to the journals *Gifted Child Quarterly* and *Parenting for High Potential*, newsletters, MemberFuse (an online community), and webinars about issues in gifted education. Special sections of the website are devoted to resources for parents, teachers, and administrators. Here are some NAGC web pages that might be especially helpful for parents:

+ **Gifted by State:** https://www.nagc.org/resources-publications/gifted-state
+ **Advocacy Toolkit:** https://www.nagc.org/get-involved/advocate-high-ability-learners/advocacy-toolkit

+ **Resources for Parents:** https://www.nagc.org/resources-publications/resources-parents

The Association for the Gifted, Council for Exceptional Children (TAG; http://cectag.org)—TAG, a division of the Council for Exceptional Children Organization, is an organization dedicated to promoting and advocating equity for gifted and talented children. TAG has developed standards for gifted educator preparation and gifted programs in partnership with NAGC. TAG's emphasis is equity in identification and services. Membership in TAG entitles you to two journals (*Journal for the Education of the Gifted* and *Excellence and Diversity in Gifted Education*), newsletters, podcasts, legislative updates, discounts, and online resources.

Supporting Emotional Needs of the Gifted (SENG; http://sengifted.org)—SENG is an organization dedicated to bringing attention to and raising awareness of the social and emotional needs of both gifted children and adults. The organization publishes free monthly newsletters and maintains a free online resource library of articles and media sources related to social and emotional issues for gifted individuals. Membership in SENG provides access to webinars, online courses, and more.

Hoagies' Gifted Education Page (http://www.hoagiesgifted.org)—Described as the website for "all things gifted," this resource contains links for students, parents, teachers, administrators, and counselors. Each link on the homepage connects to dozens of articles, books, blogs, movies, websites, magazines, and resources related to a plethora of gifted topics.

Dr. Sylvia Rimm's website (http://www.sylviarimm.com)—Mentioned several times throughout this book, this website contains numerous articles on topics such as discipline, family dynamics, underachievement, study habits, and more that apply to teachers and parents of gifted children from the preschool through teenage years. Also included are links for more information on underachievement and creativity as well as Dr. Rimm's newsletters on a variety of topics related to gifted children.

"48 Essential Links for the Parents of Gifted Children" by Open Education Database (http://oedb.org/ilibrarian/50-essen tial-links-for-the-parents-of-gifted-children)—This web page includes a wonderful collection of 48 websites, twitter accounts, blogs, and articles that provide information, resources, and advice for parents of gifted children. There is something for everyone.

#Gtchat by Texas Association of Gifted Education (http://www. txgifted.org/gtchat)—#Gtchat is a weekly Twitter chat. Join educators, parents, and guest experts in gifted education as they discuss a variety of topics, concerns, personal experiences, and resources related to gifted.

As mentioned in Chapter 1, don't forget to check out your state's department of education's website for regulations, programs, and contacts. Your school district's website should also include information about the gifted program and policies for your district.

Check out Facebook, Twitter, and the many other social media sources about gifted, but remember that anyone can create a Facebook page or a Twitter account. Always look for credible sources!

Print

If you skim through the For More Information sections in each chapter, you will notice we have mentioned many wonderful print resources from a variety of experts in the field of gifted education. We wanted to make sure, however, to highlight this book, sponsored by NAGC, as an excellent resource for parents.

Parenting Gifted Children: The Authoritative Guide from the National Association for Gifted Children **edited by Jennifer L. Jolly, Donald J. Treffinger, Tracy Ford Inman, and Joan Franklin Smutny (Prufrock Press, 2010)**—This book contains 53 articles written by experts in gifted education. The collection targets a wide range of topic related to parenting gifted children: assessment, characteristics, development, diversity, programming options, family dynamics, social and emotional needs, advocacy, and twice-exceptional students.

Several publishers specialize in the cognitive, social, and emotional needs of gifted students. Check out their websites for important resources:

+ **Corwin Press:** http://www.corwin.com
+ **The Critical Thinking Company:** http://www.criticalthinking. com
+ **Free Spirit Publishing:** http://www.freespirit.com
+ **Gifted Education Press:** http://www.giftededpress.com
+ **Great Potential Press:** http://www.greatpotentialpress.com
+ **Mind Vine Press:** http://www.mindvinepress.com
+ **Pieces of Learning:** http://www.piecesoflearning.com
+ **Routledge:** http://www.routledge.com
+ **Royal Fireworks Press:** http://www.rfwp.com

Final Thoughts

Our hope is that as you finish this book you have a better understanding of what it means for your child to be gifted, from the cognitive traits to the social and emotional issues. You know the federal and state regulations related to gifted identification and are ready to communicate with your child's school and/or district if needed. You know places to look for more information, sources for answers, and ways to find parent support or advocacy groups. And, most importantly, you know some strategies for parenting your child effectively that you can apply in both home and school situations. The more you know about giftedness, the better you are able to respond to your own child's needs, to help him develop his personal gifts and talents, and to guide her in becoming a successful, happy, productive adult. In their introduction to *Social-Emotional Curriculum with Gifted and Talented Students*, authors Joyce VanTassel-Baska, Tracy Cross, and Richard Olenchak (2009) captured the importance of validating, supporting, and guiding gifted children through the discovery of their "layers of self":

By working through the layers of self that we all bring to this thing called life, gifted students can come to know they are not alone, whether through reading about a protagonist in a novel suffering similar angst or a biography of an eminent individual who demonstrated similar struggles and came out on the other side. They can begin to express their emotions rather than repress them through the process of discussion or engagement in the arts. They can come to understand their different selves as individuals .... They can face the problems that most gifted students encounter at some stage of their growing into early adulthood—confronting perfectionism, developing important relationships, dealing with sensitivity and their own intensity, and channeling their concerns about the world into worthwhile service projects and careers. (p. 2)

But *how* do we as parents put all of this together in order to effectively validate, support, and guide our gifted children as they discover who they are? First, we ourselves strive to follow the rules in gifted educator E. Paul Torrance's Manifesto. And, then, even more importantly, we encourage our children to live by these principles!

E. Paul Torrance's Manifesto

I developed a set of guides (Torrance, 1983) for creative youngsters that Morgan Henderson and Jack Presbury called a "Manifesto" and made it into a poster that carries these words:

- Don't be afraid to "fall in love with" something and pursue it with intensity. (You will do best what you like to do most.)
- Know, understand, take pride in, practice, develop, exploit, and enjoy your greatest strengths.
- Learn to free yourself from the expectations of others and to walk away from the games they try impose on you.
- Free yourself to "play your own game" in such way as to make good use of your gifts.

E. Paul Torrance's Manifesto, continued.

- Find a great teacher or mentor who will help you.
- Don't waste a lot of expensive, unproductive energy trying to be well rounded. (Don't try to do everything; do what you can do well and what you love.)
- Learn the skills of interdependence. (Learn to depend on one another, giving freely of your greatest strengths and most intense loves.)

(Torrance, 1988, pp. 68–69)

References

Adelson, J. L. (2007). A "perfect" case study: Perfectionism in academically talented fourth graders. *Gifted Child Today, 30*(4), 14–20. doi:10.4219/gct-2007-490

Adelson, J. L., & Wilson, H. E. (2009). *Letting go of perfect: Overcoming perfectionism in kids.* Waco, TX: Prufrock Press.

Amend, E., & Peters, D. (2015). The role of a clinical psychologist: Building a comprehensive understanding of 2e students. *Gifted Child Today, 38*(4), 243–245. doi:10.1177/1076217515597286

Anonymous. (2007). Alex's gifts. *Gifted Child Today, 30*(3), 20–22. doi:10.4219/gct-2007-36

Archambault, F. X., Jr., Westberg, K. L., Brown, S. W., Hallmark, B. W., Emmons, C. L., & Zhang, W. (1993). *Regular classroom practices with gifted students: Results of a national survey of classroom teachers* (Research Monograph 93102). Storrs: University of Connecticut, The National Research Center on the Gifted and Talented.

Assouline, S. G., Colangelo, N., Lupkowski-Shoplik, A., Lipscomb, J., & Forstadt, L. (2009). *Iowa acceleration scale* (3rd ed.) Scottsdale, AZ: Great Potential Press.

Assouline, S. G., Colangelo, N., VanTassel-Baska, J., & Lupkowski-Shoplik, A. (2015). *A nation empowered: Evidence trumps the excuses holding back America's brightest students.* Iowa City: University of Iowa, The Connie Belin and Jacqueline N. Blank International Center for Gifted Education.

Baldwin, L., Baum, S., Pereles, D., & Hughes, C. (2015). Twice-exceptional learners. *Gifted Child Today*, *38*(4), 204–214. doi:10.1177/1076217515597277

Baum, S., & Novak, C. (2011). The bridges academy model in action. *2e: Twice-Exceptional Newsletter*, (45), 8–11. Retrieved from http://www.2enewsletter.com/2e_Newsletter_Issue_45.pdf

Besnoy, K. D. (2006). Successful strategies for twice-exceptional students. In F. A. Karnes & K. R. Stephens (Series Eds.), *The practical strategies series in gifted education*. Waco, TX: Prufrock Press.

Betts, G., & Islas, M. R. (2016). *Comments to ED on Title I of ESSA*. Retrieved from http://www.nagc.org/sites/default/files/Advocacy/Comments%20to%20ED%20on%20Title%20I%20of%20ESSA.pdf

Borland, J. H. (2014). Identification of gifted students. In J. A. Plucker & C. M. Callahan (Eds.), *Critical issues and practices in gifted education: What the research says* (2nd ed., pp. 323–342). Waco, TX: Prufrock Press.

Bracamonte, M. (2010). 2e students: Who they are and what they need. *2e: Twice-Exceptional Newsletter*, (39), 3–9. Retrieved from http://www.2enewsletter.com/2e_Newsletter_Issue_39.pdf

Callahan, C. M., & Hertberg-Davis, H. L. (2013). *Fundamentals of gifted education: Considering multiple perspectives.* New York, NY: Routledge.

Callahan, C. M., Moon, T. R., Oh, S., Azano, A., & Hailey, E. (2015). What works in gifted education: Documenting the effects of an integrated curricular/instructional model for gifted students. *American Educational Research Journal*, *52*, 137–167.

Colangelo, N., Assouline, S. G., & Gross, M. U. M. (2004). *A nation deceived: How schools hold back America's brightest students* (Vol. 1). Iowa City: The University of Iowa, The Connie Belin & Jacqueline N. Blank International Center for Gifted Education and Talent Development.

Coleman, M. R., & Gallagher, S. (2015). Meeting the needs of students with 2e: It takes a team. *Gifted Child Today*, *38*(4), 252–254. doi:10.1177/1076217515597274

Cross, T. L., & Betts, G. (2015). Guest forward. In S. G. Assouline, N. Colangelo, & J. VanTassel-Baska (Eds). *A nation empowered: Evidence trumps the excuses holding back America's brightest students* (Vol. 1, p. vii). Iowa City: University of Iowa, The Connie Belin & Jacqueline N. Blank International Center for Gifted Education and Development.

Davis, G. A., Rimm, S. B., & Siegle, D. (2011). *Education of the gifted and talented* (6th ed.). Upper Saddle River, NJ: Pearson.

Douglas, D. (2011). Four simple steps to self-advocacy. In J. Jolly, D. Treffinger, T. F. Inman, & J. F. Smutny (Eds.), *Parenting gifted children* (pp. 360–368). Waco, TX: Prufrock Press.

Duke TIP. (2012a). *Cognitive characteristics of gifted students: Smooth sailing, rough seas.* [Video file]. Retrieved from https://vimeo.com/41713778

Duke TIP. (2012b). *Social and emotional characteristics of gifted children: Smooth sailing, rough seas.* [Video file]. Retrieved from https://vimeo.com/41707896

Dweck, C. S. (2006). *Mindset: The new psychology of success.* New York, NY: Ballantine Books.

Every Student Succeeds Act. Pub. L. 114–95. (2015)

Ford, D.Y., & Scott, M. T. (2010). Under-representation of African American students in gifted education: Nine theories and framework for information, understanding, and change. *Gifted Education Press Quarterly, 24*(3), 2–6.

Gagné, F. (1985). Giftedness and talent: Reexamining a reexamination of the definitions. *Gifted Child Quarterly, 29*, 103–112.

Gallagher, J. J. (1975). *Teaching the gifted child* (2nd ed.). Boston, MA: Allyn & Bacon.

Gubbins, E. J. (2014). Enrichment. In J. A. Plucker & C. M. Callahan (Eds.), *Critical issues and practices in gifted education: What the research says* (pp. 223–236). Waco, TX: Prufrock Press.

Henderson, A., Jacob, B., Kernan-Schloss, A., & Raimondo, B. (2004). *The case for parent leadership.* Lexington, KY: Pritchard Committee for Academic Excellence.

Individuals with Disabilities Education Act, 20 U.S.C. § 1400 (2004).

Inman, T. F. (2015). What a child doesn't learn . . . . In J. L. Roberts & T. F. Inman, *Strategies for differentiating instruction: Best practices in the classroom* (3rd ed., pp. 205–209). Waco, TX: Prufrock Press.

Javits act funding history. (2014). Retrieved from http://commons. trincoll.edu/wp-content/blogs.dir/67/files/2014/05/Sheet1.pdf

Jensen, E. (2006). *Enriching the brain: How to maximize every learner's potential.* San Francisco, CA: John Wiley & Sons.

Kerr, B. (2015). *Creativity and STEM.* Session presented at 2015 Wedge Annual Speaker Series, Bowling Green, KY.

Lind, S. (2001). Overexcitability and the gifted. *SENG Newsletter, 1*(1), 3–6. Retrieved from http://sengifted.org/archives/articles/ overexcitability-and-the-gifted

Loveless, T., Farkas, S., & Duffett, A. (Eds). (2008). *High-achieving students in the era of NCLB.* Washington, DC: Thomas B. Fordham Institute. Retrieved from http://edexcellence.net/publications/ high-achieving-students-in.html

Marland, S. P. (1972). *Education of the gifted and talented, Volume 1.* Report to the Congress of the United States by the U.S. Commissioner of Education. Washington, DC: U.S. Government Printing Office.

McCoach, D. B., & Siegle, D. (2008). Underachievers. In J. A. Plucker & C. M Callahan (Eds.), *Critical issues and practices in gifted education: What the research says* (pp. 721–734). Waco, TX: Prufrock Press.

McCoach, D. B., & Siegle, D. (2014). Underachievers. In J. A. Plucker & C. M Callahan (Eds.), *Critical issues and practices in gifted education: What the research says* (2nd ed., pp. 691–706). Waco, TX: Prufrock Press.

McCombs, B. (2010). *Developing responsible and autonomous learners: A key to motivating students.* American Psychological Association. Retrieved from http://www.apa.org/education/k12/learners.aspx

Moon, S. (2009). Myth 15: High-ability students don't face problems and challenges. *Gifted Child Quarterly, 53*(4), 274–276.

National Association for Gifted Children. (2009). *White paper: Twice exceptionality.* Washington, DC: Author. Retrieved from http:// www.nagc.org/sites/default/files/Position%20Statement/twice%20 exceptional.pdf

National Association for Gifted Children. (2010). *NAGC Pre-K–Grade 12 Gifted Programming Standards: A blueprint for quality gifted education programs.* Washington, DC: Author.

National Association for Gifted Children. (2015a). *2014–2015 State of the nation in gifted education.* Washington, DC: Author. Retrieved from http://www.nagc.org/sites/default/ files/key%20 reports/2014-2015%20State%20of%20the%20States%20 %28final%29.pdf

National Association for Gifted Children. (2015b). *Questions and answers about the Every Student Succeeds Act (ESSA).* Retrieved from http://www.nagc.org/sites/default/files/Advocacy/ESSA%20Q%20 %2B%20A.pdf

National Association for Gifted Children & The Council of State Directors of Programs for the Gifted. (2015). *2014–2015 State of the states in gifted education: Policy and practice data summary.* Washington, DC: Author. Retrieved from http://www.nagc.org/ sites/default/files/key%20reports/2014-2015%20State%20of%20 the%20States%20 summary.pdf

New Teacher Center. (2015). About TELL. *Tell Resource Library.* Retrieved from http://teachingconditions.org/home/about-tell

No Child Left Behind Act, 20 USC 7801 (2004).

Passow, A. H. (1982). Differentiated curricula for the gifted/talented: A point of view. In S. Kaplan, A.H. Passow, P.H. Phenix, S. Reis, J. S. Renzulli, I. Sato, L. Smith, E. P. Torrance, & V.S. Ward. *Curricula for the gifted* (pp. 4–20). Ventura, CA: National/State Leadership Training Institute on the Gifted/Talented.

Piechowski, M. M. (1991). Emotional development and emotional giftedness. In N. Colangelo & G. A. Davis (Eds.), *Handbook of gifted education* (pp. 285–306). Boston, MA: Allyn & Bacon.

Plucker, J. A., (2011). *Mind the excellence gap!* Session presented at Western Kentucky University's Victoria Fellows Program, Bowling Green, KY.

Plucker, J. A., Burroughs, N., & Song, R. (2010). *Mind the (other) gap: The growing excellence gap in K–12 education.* Bloomington: Indiana University, Center for Evaluation and Education Policy. Retrieved from http://ceep.indiana.edu/mindthegap/mind.html

Plucker, J. A., Hardesty, J., & Burroughs, N. (2013). *Talent on the sidelines: Excellence gaps and America's persistent talent underclass.* Storrs: University of Connecticut, Center for Education Policy Analysis at the Neag School of Education. Retrieved from http://webdev.education.uconn.edu/static/sites/cepa/AG/excellence2013/Excellence-Gap-10-18-13_JP_LK.pdf

Reis, S., & McCoach, B. (2000). The underachievement of gifted students: What we know and where do we go?. *Gifted Child Quarterly, 44*(3), 152–170.

Renzulli, J. S. (1978). What makes giftedness? Re-examining a definition. *Phi Delta Kappa, 60,* 180–181.

Renzulli, J. S., & Reis, S. M. (2014). *The Schoolwide Enrichment Model: A how-to guide for educational excellence* (3rd ed.). Waco, TX: Prufrock Press.

Ricci, M. C. (2013). *Mindsets in the classroom: Building a culture of success and student achievement in school.* Waco, TX: Prufrock Press.

Ricci, M. C. (2015). *Ready-to-use resources for mindsets in the classroom.* Waco, TX: Prufrock Press.

Rimm, S. B. (1997). An underachievement epidemic. *Educational Leadership, 54*(7), 18–22.

Rimm, S. B. (2008). *Why bright kids get poor grades and what you can do about it: A six-step program for parents and teachers.* Scottsdale, AZ: Great Potential Press.

Rimm, S. B. (2010). *How to parent so children will learn: Top ten list.* Retrieved from http://www.sylviarimm.com/article_htp.html

Roberts, J. L. (2005). Enrichment opportunities for gifted learners. In F. A. Karnes & K. R. Stephens (Series Eds.), *The practical strategies series in gifted education.* Waco, TX: Prufrock Press.

Roberts, J. L. (2016). Letter from Julia. *The Challenge, 38,* 2. Retrieved from http://www.wku.edu/gifted/resources/the_challenge.php

Roberts, J. L., & Inman, T. F. (2009, June). Advocacy column: Communicating powerful and timely advocacy messages. *Parenting for High Potential,* 9–11.

Roberts, J. L., & Inman, T. F. (2011). Effective advocates, lifelong advocacy: If not you, then who? In J. Jolly, D. Treffinger, T. F. Inman, &

J. F. Smutny (Eds.), *Parenting gifted children* (pp. 327–331). Waco, TX: Prufrock Press.

Roberts, J. L., & Inman, T. F. (2013). *Teacher's survival guide: Differentiating instruction in the elementary classroom.* Waco, TX: Prufrock Press.

Roberts, J. L., & Inman, T. F. (2015). *Strategies for differentiating instruction: Best practices in the classroom* (3rd ed.). Waco, TX: Prufrock Press.

Roberts, J. L., Pereira, N., & Knotts, J. D. (2015, October.) State law and policy related to twice-exceptional learners. *Gifted Child Today, 38*(4), 215–219. doi: 10.1177/1076217515597276

Robinson, N. M., Reis, S. M., Neihart, M., & Moon, S. M. (2002). *The social and emotional development of gifted children: What do we know?* Waco, TX: Prufrock Press.

Rogers, K. B. (2006). *A menu of options for grouping gifted students.* Waco, TX: Prufrock Press.

Rogers, K. B. (2014). Why would you group the gifted? Making it practical. Keynote presented at the annual conference of the Kentucky Association for Gifted Education, Lexington, KY.

Rogers, K. B. (2015). The academic, socialization, and psychological effects of acceleration: Research synthesis. In S. G. Assouline, N. Colangelo, J. VanTassel-Baska & A. Lupkowski-Shoplik (Eds.), *A nation empowered: Evidence trumps the excuses holding back America's brightest students* (Vol. 2) (pp. 19–29). Iowa City: University of Iowa, The Connie Belin & Jacqueline N. Blank International Center for Gifted Education and Development.

Rothstein, D., & Santana, L. (2014). *Make just one change: Teach students to ask their own questions.* Cambridge, MA: Harvard Education Press.

Schunk, D. H. (1987). Peer models and children's behavioral change. *Review of Educational Research, 57,* 149–174.

Siegle, D. (2004). Living up to their potential: Strategies for promoting achievement-oriented students. *Gifted Education Communicator, 35*(4), 31–35.

Siegle, D. (2007). *Gifted children's bill of rights*. Retrieved from http://www.nagc.org/resources-publications/resources-parents/gifted-childrens-bill-rights

Siegle, D., & McCoach, B. (2008). Issues related to the underachievement of gifted students. In B. MacFarlane & T. Stambaugh (Eds.), *Leading change in gifted education: The festschrift of Dr. Joyce VanTassel-Baska*. Waco, TX: Prufrock Press.

Silverman, L. (n.d.). Emotional intensity. Gifted Development Center. Retrieved from http://www.skitsap.wednet.edu/cms/lib/WA01000495/Centricity/Domain/1914/Understanding%20Gifted%20-%20Fisher.pdf

Silverman, L. K. (2009). Petunias, perfectionism, and level of development. In S. Daniels, & M. Piechowski (Eds.), *Living with intensity* (pp. 145–164). Scottsdale, AZ: Great Potential Press.

Smutny, J. F. (2011a). Characteristics and development. In J. Jolly, D. Treffinger, T. F. Inman, & J. F. Smutny (Eds.), *Parenting gifted children* (pp. 37–41). Waco, TX: Prufrock Press.

Smutny, J. F. (2011b). Differentiated instruction for young gifted children: How parents can help. In J. Jolly, D. Treffinger, T. F. Inman, and J. F. Smutny (Eds.), *Parenting gifted children* (pp. 221–233). Waco, TX: Prufrock Press.

Southern, W. T., & Jones, E. D. (2015) Types of acceleration: Dimensions and issues. In S. G. Assouline, N. Colangelo, J. VanTassel-Baska, & A. Lupkowski-Shoplik (Eds.), *A nation empowered: Evidence trumps the excuses holding back America's brightest students* (Vol. 2) (pp. 9–18). Iowa City: University of Iowa, The Connie Belin & Jacqueline N. Blank International Center for Gifted Education and Development.

Subotnik, R., Olszewski-Kubilius, P., & Worrell, F. (2011). Rethinking giftedness and gifted education: A proposed direction forward based on psychological science. *Psychological Science in the Public Interest, 12*(1), 3–54. doi: 10.1177/1529100611418056

Sword, L. K. (n.d.) Emotional intensity in gifted children. *SENG Newsletter*. Retrieved from http://sengifted.org/archives/articles/emotional-intensity-in-gifted-children.

TELL Colorado. (2015). Result details. Retrieved from http://www.tellcolorado.org/results

TELL Kentucky. (2015). Result details. Retrieved from http://www.tellkentucky.org/results

TELL Maryland. (2015). Result details. Retrieved from http://www.tellmaryland.org/results

TELL Tennessee. (2015). Result details. Retrieved from http://telltennessee.org/results

Tomlinson, C. A., & Imbeau, M. (2010). *Leading and managing a differentiated classroom.* Alexandria, VA: Association for Supervision and Curriculum Development.

Torrance, E. P. (1988). Creativity as manifest in testing. In R. L. Sternberg (Ed.), *The nature of creativity: Contemporary psychological perspectives* (pp. 43–75). Cambridge, England: Cambridge University Press.

Treffinger, D. (2009). Guest editorial. *Gifted Child Quarterly, 53*(4), 229–232.

U.S. Department of Education. (2010). Thirty-five years of progress in educating children with disabilities through IDEA. Retrieved from http://www2.ed.gov/about/offices/list/osers/idea35/history/idea-35-history.pdf

University of Washington. (2015). What is the difference between an iep and a 504 plan? Retrieved from http://www.washington.edu/doit/what-difference-between-iep-and-504-plan

VanTassel-Baska, J. L., Cross, T. L., & Olenchak, F. R. (Eds.). (2009). *Social-emotional curriculum with gifted and talented students.* Waco, TX: Prufrock Press.

Wai, J. (2015). Long-term effects of educational acceleration In S. G. Assouline, N. Colangelo, & J. VanTassel-Baska (Eds.), *A nation empowered: Evidence trumps the excuses holding back America's brightest students* (Vol. 1) (pp. 73–84). Iowa City: University of Iowa, The Connie Belin & Jacqueline N. Blank International Center for Gifted Education and Development.

Walker, S. Y. (2002). *The survival guide for parents of gifted kids.* Minneapolis, MN: Free Spirit.

Webb, J. T., Amend, E. R., Webb, N. E., Goerss, J., Beljan, P. & Olenchak, F. R. (2005). *Misdiagnosis and dual diagnoses of gifted children and adults: ADHD, bipolar, OCD, Asperger's, depression, and other disorders.* Scottsdale, AZ: Great Potential Press.

Webb, J. T., Gore, J. L., Amend, E. R., & DeVries, A. (2007). *A parent's guide to gifted children.* Scottsdale, AZ: Great Potential Press.

Wechsler Intelligence Scale for Children®–Fifth Edition. (2014). San Antonio, TX: Pearson.

Westberg, K. L., & Daoust, M. E. (2003, Fall). The results of the replication of the Classroom Practices Survey replication in two states. *The National Research Center on the Gifted and Talented Newsletter.* Storrs: University of Connecticut, The National Research Center on the Gifted and Talented.

Wiley, K., & Brunner, M. M. (2014). Nonverbal assessment and identification. In J. A. Plucker & C. M. Callahan (Eds.), *Critical issues and practices in gifted education: What the research says* (2nd ed., pp. 465–479). Waco, TX: Prufrock Press.

Worrell, F. (2009). Myth 4: Single test score or indicator tells us all we need to know about giftedness. *Gifted Child Quarterly, 53*(4), 242–244.

Glossary

Acceleration: The process where students move at a faster pace through a specific content or grade level than age-based peers (Chapter 5).

+ *Content-based acceleration*: Progressing through the curriculum faster (e.g., sixth-grade math) and moving to the next level (e.g., seventh-grade math) but staying with the same age peers throughout the day.

+ *Grade-based acceleration*: Typically involves a student graduating before her age-based peers (e.g., skipping an entire year such as going from third to fifth grade or gaining early entrance into kindergarten, middle school, high school, or college).

Asynchronous development: Different aspects of children develop at different rates, for instance cognitive development may occur faster than fine motor skills, or math ability may progress faster than social skills (Chapter 3).

Cluster grouping: A type of grouping where five to eight top-performing students in an area or students identified as gifted in an area are grouped in the same class and receive differentiated learning experiences (Chapter 5).

Cooperative grouping: A type of grouping where high performing students or students identified as gifted are grouped together to work cooperatively on a specific task (Chapter 5).

Curriculum compacting: A type of acceleration where a student (after taking a preassessment) studies only the content or skills not known in the unit of study (Chapter 5).

Differentiation: The deliberate, intentionally planned matching of the content, thinking processes, and/or products to the needs, interests, or readiness levels of the child (Chapter 5).

Disability: Mental retardation, a hearing impairment (including deafness), a speech or language impairment, a visual impairment (including blindness), a serious emotional disturbance, an orthopedic impairment, autism, traumatic brain injury, another health impairment, a specific learning disability, deaf-blindness, or multiple disabilities; needs special education and related services (Chapter 9).

Effect size: Statistic that indicates the size of the difference a treatment has between two groups (Chapter 5).

Enrichment: Lessons, strategies, or activities provided for students that supplement or go beyond the grade-level work (Chapter 5).

Excellence gap: Term coined by Jonathan Plucker that describes the discrepancies in achievement between students from high poverty or ethnically diverse backgrounds and their more advantaged peers (Chapter 6).

Intelligence Quotient (IQ): Score from a standardized test that represents the general intelligence of a person (Chapter 1).

Gifted and talented:

+ *Marland Report (1972)*: Children with outstanding abilities who are capable of high performance.

+ *Every Student Succeeds Act (2015)*: Children who give evidence of high achievement capability in intellectual, creative, artistic, or leadership capacity, or in specific academic fields, and who need extra services to develop those capabilities.

+ *Subotnik, Olszewski-Kubilius, & Worrell (2011)*: The manifestation of performance or production that is clearly at the upper end of the distribution in a talent domain even relative to that of other high-functioning individuals in that domain; giftedness can be viewed as developmental (Chapter 1).

Grouping: Placing learners in specific combinations of students who have similar needs, interests, readiness levels, etc. in order to better meet needs; instruction varies based on needs (Chapter 5).

+ *Ability grouping*: Combines students who score similarly on some sort of aptitude or achievement assessment.

+ *Performance grouping*: Combines students with similar grades or levels of performance.

Identification: Process of determining exceptionalities in learners; should involve multiple, valid measures including verbal and nonverbal assessments, portfolios, check lists, etc. (Chapter 1 and Chapter 6).

Meta-analysis: Statistical technique involving the combination of studies done on a topic (Chapter 2 and Chapter 5).

Mindset: Concept developed by psychologist Carol Dweck that deals with how a person views intelligence or talent (Chapter 4).

+ *Fixed mindset*: Belief that intelligence, abilities, and talents are predetermined in a person (i. e., you are just born with it).

+ *Growth mindset*: Belief that a person's intelligence, abilities, or talents can be developed with effort and persistence.

Overexcitability: An intense emotion or heightened response to a stimuli often expressed by gifted children: psychomotor (always being on the move and full of energy); sensual (heightened awareness to sight, smell, touch, taste, and sound); intellectual (a strong desire to understand hows and whys and/or a passion for a certain topic of interest); imaginational (heightened sense of creativity or imagination); emotional (ability to experience complex motions and/or a heightened sense of compassion or empathy; Chapter 4).

Perfectionism: Desire to be exemplary in all ways; can be healthy (e.g., setting challenging goals and working hard to master those goals) or unhealthy (being too competitive with a focus on winning and self-criticism when things don't go as planned; Chapter 4).

Preassessment: Any type of assessment given before a unit of study to determine students' prior knowledge and mastery of the content or skills (Chapter 5).

Pull-out program: Students gifted in the same area are pulled from class by a trained teacher to work on extensions of content, critical thinking skills, or creativity (Chapter 5).

Self-paced instruction: Type of acceleration where the student moves through the content at his own pace based on mastery of the standards (Chapter 5).

Service: Educational option designed to address the needs, interests, and abilities of the student; these include differentiation in the regular classroom, acceleration, dual credit, independent study, and more (Chapter 5 and Chapter 6).

Stanine: Measurement used in standardized testing that is a 9-point sale, with 5 being average (Chapter 1).

Twice-exceptional: Learners with gifts and talents who also have another exceptionality such as a learning disability (Chapter 9).

Underachievement: Substantial discrepancy between a student's ability to achieve (based on IQ or standardized tests) and her actual achievement (Chapter 6).

About the Authors

Tracy Ford Inman, Ed. D., is associate director of The Center for Gifted Studies at Western Kentucky University and active on the state, national, and international levels in gifted education. She has taught English at the high school and collegiate levels, as well as in summer programs for gifted and talented youth. In addition to writing and cowriting several articles, Tracy has coauthored three books with Julia Roberts through Prufrock Press: *Strategies for Differentiating Instruction: Best Practices for the Classroom*, now in its third edition, *Assessing Differentiated Student Products: A Protocol for Development and Evaluation* (2nd ed.), and *Teacher's Survival Guide: Differentiating Instruction in the Elementary Classroom*. Tracy and Julia received the Legacy Book Award from the Texas Association for the Gifted and Talented for Strategies for Differentiating Instruction. Tracy was coeditor of *Parenting Gifted Children: The Authoritative Guide from the National Association for Gifted Children*, a compilation of the best articles in *Parenting for High Potential*, which won the Legacy Book Award in 2011.

Jana Kirchner, Ph.D., is the Instructional Supervisor for Simpson County Schools in Franklin, KY. She has 26 years of experience in education, which includes being an assistant professor in the School of Teacher Education at Western Kentucky University, a social studies consultant, an ACT Quality Core facilitator, and a high school English and social studies teacher. She earned her Ph.D. in educational leadership, with an emphasis in curriculum and instruction, from the

University of Louisville. She has provided professional development, coached teachers, presented at state and national conferences, coauthored *Inquiry-Based Lessons in U.S. History: Decoding the Past* with Dr. Andrew McMichael, and written articles and book chapters on social studies, differentiation, content literacy, and teaching strategies.

Printed in the United States
by Baker & Taylor Publisher Services